MW01074561

The New Science of Momentum

The
New Science
of
Momentum

How the Best Coaches and Leaders
Build a Fire from a Single Spark

DON YAEGER AND BERNARD BANKS
WITH KAREN CYPHERS

HARPERCOLLINS
LEADERSHIP

AN IMPRINT OF HARPERCOLLINS

Design by Neuwirth & Associates, Inc.

ISBN 978-1-4002-4719-6 (eBook)
ISBN 978-1-4002-4713-4 (HC)
ISBN 978-1-4002-5423-1 (TP)

Library of Congress Control Number: 2025931637

Printed in the United States of America
25 26 27 28 29 LBC 5 4 3 2 1

Jeanette, Will, and Maddie:
Adding you to my life has given me momentum I could never have
imagined. Thank you for being the team that makes everything possible
and the journey worth taking!
DY

I dedicate this book to the family, friends, and colleagues
who have inspired me throughout the years.
BBB

Contents

CONTENTS

Introduction

During the first quarter of Super Bowl LI in February 2017, the Nielsen Company estimated two hundred million viewers around the globe were tuned to their televisions, ready for that year's most-watched sporting event. By the third quarter, nearly half the audience was gone. The Atlanta Falcons were pounding the favored New England Patriots, and few outside of Georgia's capital city wanted to watch a rout.

Through the first half, everything that could go right for the Falcons did. Conversely, New England was not much fun to watch, with quarterback Tom Brady getting sacked multiple times, throwing incomplete passes to wide open receivers, and nightmare of all nightmares for a Bill Belichick team, making silly mistakes like fumbling a handoff to running back LeGarrette Blount that the Falcons converted into a touchdown soon after. Even when the Falcons faltered, as they did during the final seven minutes of the first half, the hapless Pats could manage only a field goal. Three points. That was all the scoring the high-powered New England offense registered during the first thirty minutes of play.

"In football you're always playing for what we call the second half swing," Patriots cornerback Devin McCourty said in an interview for this book. "That's where you want to get the ball and go down and score just before halftime, then get it again to start the second half and score again. You take over the momentum of the game and the other team feels like they are done. For us in that game, it was the complete opposite."

Coming out of the locker room, the Falcons scored again and, midway through the third quarter, led New England 28–3. "If you're New England, that's not what you want to see," announcer Joe Buck said, as the camera zoomed to Belichick deadpanning on the sideline.

No, it was not.

"I was sitting on the sidelines saying to myself you are getting your butt embarrassed," Brady recalled years later. "Go out and do something. Let's just get one touchdown."

And then a small victory came New England's way. On third down with eight yards to go, Brady was forced out of the pocket— always an uneasy moment for Patriots fans—but scrambled convincingly for a first down. A few plays later, he threw a short touchdown pass to running back James White to make it 28–9. The crowd cheered but, at this point, the outcome still seemed foregone. The Patriots missed the extra point, but at least the score seemed a bit more respectable.

"Once we scored, I asked the defense to just get one stop, just one," Brady said. "They did and then we drove the field and kicked a field goal." There was 9:44 left in the game. "I looked over at the scoreboard and said it was only a two-score game."

Just over a minute of game time later, with Atlanta still leading 28–12, Falcons quarterback Matt Ryan dropped back to pass and was engulfed by Patriot linebacker Dont'a Hightower, causing Ryan to fumble. The Patriots recovered the ball on the Falcons' 25-yard line.

"That strip sack by Dont'a was the moment when you could feel it turn," McCourty said. "In that moment, we all looked at each other and said, 'We can win this game.' Guys on both sides of the ball started making plays off the energy we gained from that one play and the belief was on our side."

"You felt it," Brady said. "We had some juice. Those little plays were becoming a snowball."

Not long after that, Brady found Danny Amendola in the end zone for a touchdown. Immediately, Belichick lifted two fingers, signaling his team was going for two points. They earned the two with a classic bit of Belichickian deception as the ball was directly snapped to White (rather than Brady), who converted. Suddenly, the score was 28–20 and, with just under six minutes to play, the contest that seemed out of reach was anybody's game. At that point, a change was noticeable when looking at the body language of players on both teams. McCourty summed it up: "When we were only down by a touchdown, their players . . . their eyes started to get big. They knew we were coming. They knew we had Tom Brady and no one wants to be in a one-score game if he's on the other side. Our eyes, they started to narrow. We were locked in. It was a complete reversal of the first three-and-a-half quarters. They had a special teams player who, for most of the game, was barking at our sideline, talking trash after every kickoff. When we were down only one score, you could see him turn quietly after the kickoff and just jog off the field. Now we're the ones screaming. What people don't realize is that there are so many defensive players on the kickoff that the energy flows right into the next play as their offense comes out. And both sides know it. You both feel it. It's almost like an out-of-body experience."

With four minutes remaining in the game, Atlanta moved the ball to the New England 22-yard line, close enough for a field goal that would make any further New England comeback unlikely. But once again the Patriots defense answered the call. McCourty tackled a Falcons ball carrier for a loss, then Trey Flower sacked Ryan back near the 40-yard line. On the next play, the New England defense's pressure forced one of the Atlanta linemen into a penalty, pushing the ball back yet farther. The Falcons were certainly moving the ball ... the problem was they were moving it in the wrong direction.

The Patriots forced the Falcons to punt and recovered the punt just inside their own 10-yard line. They had a little over three minutes to go ninety yards for a touchdown, after which they had to go for two again. Brady completed three passes in a row to three different players. One tripped and fell running his route, got up, and still made the catch. Another, Julian Edelman, had the pass tipped in front of him, making the pass available to the outstretched hands of no fewer than three Falcons players who converged on the ball.

Game over.

Except it wasn't. Somehow, Edelman snaked his way among them and came up with the catch, the replay showing that his concentration was so absolute you could see him pin the ball against the opponent's leg to keep it off the ground, where it would have been ruled incomplete.

With one minute left to play, White ran for a touchdown to bring the Patriots within two points of the Falcons. During the two-point conversion, a Falcons lineman jumped offsides but still couldn't prevent Edelman from catching a short screen pass and stretching the ball over the goal line. At this point, those watching the game were witnessing the greatest Super Bowl comeback of all time.

"The energy is so completely with New England," Aikman said. "This has been two completely different games. I don't have any idea how the Falcons respond in overtime."

They didn't get the chance. The Patriots won the coin toss and chose to receive the ball first. Now well protected by his offensive line, Brady proceeded to pick apart the Falcons' defense and brought the Patriots to a first and goal after a Falcon defender was whistled for pass interference in the end zone. Two plays later, White ran it in for yet another New England Super Bowl victory.

As the confetti fell like snow on the players and the crowds who rushed onto the field, a national radio announcer summed it up, saying: "Final score is 34–28 in overtime, and the New England Patriots have redefined the word *momentum* here tonight."

The next morning, this book was born when a sports author gathered a team in Florida, turned to a large whiteboard, and scribbled the words *How does a team turn a moment into momentum?* Over the next seven-plus years, the project would grow to include a retired Army general whose last duty assignment was to serve as the chair of the Department of Behavioral Sciences and Leadership at the US Military Academy at West Point; a highly respected research scientist from the world of academics; and one of the best data analysts working in the worlds of public opinion and politics. The list of questions on the whiteboard grew: How do you prepare for "the moment"? Can momentum be generated? Can it be extended? What can be done if it has turned against you?

Hundreds of interviews with and thousands of surveys of world-renowned experts, championship coaches, military leaders, political campaign strategists, and corporate leaders conducted over the past few years led us to the words you hold today.

One thing became clear: Momentum is real to those we sought to learn from. How to prepare for, manipulate, extend, or reverse it became our assignment. This book will provide you with a model to do exactly that.

So, use the energy from that sentence to propel you to the next chapter. Let's go!

The New Science of Momentum

1

Premise:
From Flow to Mo

When Mihaly Csikszentmihalyi began exploring his theory of "flow," he was called crazy, a crackpot. The venerable professor and researcher was convinced that people who found themselves in "flow" were able to stay focused longer and were thus capable of greater things. He knew he had felt it while he was writing. He knew he had seen it among athletes who seemingly come to a place where they can't miss. But when he proposed this idea that "flow" was a "state" and should be pursued, his professional colleagues originally scoffed.

Thirty years later, Csikszentmihalyi's seminal book *Flow: The Psychology of Optimal Experience* is not only widely accepted but a bestseller that is celebrated as one of the most transformative theories in the psychology of performance. We were lucky for a chance to sit down with him for a lengthy dinner interview, prior to his passing in 2021, where he shared his thoughts on the evolution of "flow" and debated with us the intersection of this concept with momentum—both in the experiences of individuals and for teams.

Flow state has gained a great deal of attention recently as biohackers seek ways to tap into this state of intense creativity and productivity, particularly for individuals seeking to maximize performance. What has long been known to athletes as "being in the zone," flow state is now widely recognized as a phenomenon in no way limited to sports but an almost-euphoric sense of possibility and accomplishment with little sense of time, limitations, or practical constraints.

Flow states have implications for teams, as well as individuals. Emerging science is beginning to prove something that has long been theorized: the existence of "mirror neurons," which seem to be the basis for human empathy and intuition. These are the chemical messengers that transmit anticipated actions and evoke automatic responses from those around us. A simple example: How often have you felt like yawning after watching one or two others do so? But in a larger sense, mirror neurons seem to be the key to how any kind of collective emotion—excitement, hysteria, momentum—spreads organically through a group. The study of mirror neurons is at the cutting edge of neurological research and has the potential to redefine the way we understand the social aspect of the human brain.

Transference of energy is one of the key properties of creating momentum in physics; it is also the secret to building momentum within a team. But how does this process happen? Enter mirror neurons as one possibility. As one team member begins to experience success, the mirror neurons of their teammates begin to register those accomplishments as their own. Combined with procedural adaptation and an understanding of body language, the receptivity of mirror neurons can help make momentum contagious—and virtually unstoppable. Our interviews with neuroscientists Marco Iacoboni and Jaime Pineda detail the process where as one person achieves something positive, the psychological impact of tribal identity ("you are in my group, which means that you are like me and aligned with my goals") triggers a verifiable, biological mental response in teammates. If teammates are properly aligned, their mirror neurons respond to the victory as if they, too, had successfully completed the task. This creates a kind of "mental muscle memory" within the brain, triggering growing confidence and feelings of accomplishment within the entire group. It is this kind of contagious success that becomes momentum.

Csikszentmihalyi embraced as an extension of individual flow states our model of momentum, which is focused on how organizations can foster environments in which momentum can easily be transferred from one to another.

"The role of the leader or the coach is to be aware, to know what the strengths of the set of individuals are and to recognize the opportunity for using those strengths in the activity that you are doing together," Csikszentmihalyi told us, agreeing that the experience of "flow" is transferable between members of an organization—"if they are in synchrony and supporting each other. And things like faith are very important."

Csikszentmihalyi conducted extensive research to develop the ideas presented in *Flow*. His research methods were rigorous and innovative, particularly in how he gathered data from participants. One of the key methods he used was the Experience Sampling Method (ESM), which involved having participants keep detailed daily logs or journals about their experiences throughout the day. Participants were provided with pagers or other devices (in later studies, they used smartphones) that would alert them at random times throughout the day. When signaled, participants were asked to stop what they were doing and fill out a short survey or journal entry. In these entries, participants recorded what they were doing at that moment, how they felt, their level of concentration, and their overall sense of engagement or satisfaction with the activity. This method allowed Csikszentmihalyi to gather real-time data on people's experiences, rather than relying on retrospective accounts.

In addition to the real-time sampling, participants were sometimes asked to keep more detailed journals about their experiences, particularly those that involved deep concentration or enjoyment, to help identify patterns in how flow experiences occurred. Csikszentmihalyi analyzed the data from these logs and journals to identify common conditions that facilitated the flow state. He found that flow experiences often occurred when individuals were engaged in activities that were challenging but achievable, where they had clear goals and immediate feedback, and where they were fully absorbed in the task at hand.

The insights gained from these detailed logs were crucial in shaping the concept of flow. Csikszentmihalyi was able to define flow as a state where individuals are so engrossed in an activity that they lose track of time and self-consciousness, finding deep satisfaction in the process itself. This ESM method not only was instrumental in developing Csikszentmihalyi's "flow" but has since been widely applied in psychology, education, sports, and many other fields.

Our research for this book also involved the solicitation of people's thoughts, feelings, and experiences with personal and team momentum, via three alternative methods: in-depth interviews; targeted surveys of leaders in business, politics, sports, and the military; and large-scale, scientific surveys of the general public.

In all of these surveys and interviews, we asked: "Does momentum exist?" A staggering number said yes, it does. This was the answer for 91 percent of the twenty-five-hundred-plus Americans we asked in random sample surveys, and for an even greater portion—99 percent of the thousand coaches, business leaders, and National War College military officers we targeted in our surveys of leaders. There were, of course, a few outliers—including an ESPN statistician who argued vociferously that momentum is an artifact or fallacy rather than a real phenomenon. That said, our research found that the more groups or teams a person has been a member of, the more likely they are to state a belief in the realness of momentum. More on that later. For now, it's clear that nearly everyone we contacted believed they had lived momentum in some context and perhaps fallen victim to it as well. Pressed to define momentum outside of a feeling, however, no uniform descriptions emerged. Our respondents offered diverse descriptions, with professionals in these four fields—politics, sports, the military, and business—providing particularly colorful ones of the phenomenon.

Florida State University assistant basketball coach Stan Jones described momentum to us as a "competitive energy tsunami," a powerful surge that propels a team forward, elevating their performance beyond expectations. In our talk with acclaimed leadership expert John Maxwell, he described momentum as the "great exaggerator," magnifying existing currents and intensifying their impact. And perhaps most vividly, NBA champion assistant coach Kevin Eastman told us he thinks of momentum as a "force multiplier"—that momentum is "the force of energy, the force of enthusiasm, the force of *we're coming at you.*"

Defining momentum may be like trying to catch lightning in a bottle—it's something you can feel, but it's elusive when you try to put it into words. You can feel things shift, but it's challenging to quantify or measure. The debate over momentum even served as the reason one major figure, legendary political consultant James Carville, decided to participate in this book. "Momentum is absolutely real. I think it's a noble thing you're doing in writing this book," Carville said, before qualifying his reason for offering such a superlative. "I think it's noble because you're going to try to explain something and you're going to fail, but I just don't want you to fail too big." He made it clear he was offering a little of his trademark sarcasm but was fascinated enough that he invited the authors to spend a day with him at his Virginia home.

These individuals, at the pinnacle of their fields, share a visceral understanding of momentum through their firsthand experiences. Their ability to articulate its essence suggests that those who have been deeply immersed in the ebbs and flows of competitive environments are more attuned to its effects.

These professionals weren't coached or taught about how to describe momentum; rather, the largely common experience of this phenomenon led to a remarkably similar view: When momentum is happening, captured energy is released with a greater yield than expected.

Momentum magnifies.

While those at the tops of their respective fields may have seen and felt momentum in their personal lives more than the average person, in our surveys of American adults, more than eight in ten say they've experienced it firsthand too.

Perhaps most telling, however, is the wide gap between the belief in momentum and a confident understanding of what contributes to it. Nearly nine in ten respondents in our surveys say they believe certain conditions can help create momentum or make it more likely to occur; but when asked to elaborate on what those conditions might be, most said they aren't sure.

This book explores those conditions and how to build them. But first, it's important to start with the basics: the scientific basis and definition of momentum, concepts that are related to but distinct from momentum, and an exploration of some efforts to "catch" or measure "Mo" in social contexts.

2

Momentum
Defined

"**T**ry to define it."

Try to define love or pornography. Supreme Court Justice Potter Stewart tried with the latter but defaulted to what became among the best-known phrases in US legal history: "I know it when I see it."

Momentum joins the list of phenomena that can be perceived more easily than described. And it's described . . . a lot.

Think of the number of idioms that allude to momentum: "keep the ball rolling"; "gather steam"; "hit one's stride"; "in full swing"; "gain traction"; "ride the wave"; "snowball effect"; "run with it."

And, of course, there are various clichés that dance around the same concept: "strike while the iron is hot," "a rolling stone gathers no moss," "the more you do, the more you can do," "stay in the flow," "success breeds success." It's no surprise, then, that most people believe—perhaps even without having consciously considered the question—that momentum is real.

Most come to understand momentum long before they learn there's a word for what such an experience feels like. Indeed, the concept becomes a lot easier to explain when you've felt it yourself—and more importantly, when you've been given the tools to spot it when it's happening and to prepare for that moment.

In physics, momentum—that is, transferred energy—is a property of a moving object that's defined as the product of its mass and velocity. It is a vector quantity, meaning it has both magnitude and direction. The formula for momentum is:

$$\text{Momentum} = \text{Mass} \times \text{Velocity}$$

Here's what each part means:

- Momentum: This tells us how much "push" an object has when it's moving. If something has more momentum, it means it's harder to stop.

- Mass: This is how much stuff is in the object, like how heavy it is. The more mass an object has, the more momentum it can have.

- Velocity: This is how fast the object is moving and in what direction. The faster something moves, the more momentum it has.

In other words, in physics, momentum depends on both the mass and the velocity of an object. An object with a greater mass or a higher velocity will have greater momentum. For example, a truck moving at a high speed will have a greater momentum than a bicycle moving at the same speed. Beyond mass and velocity, there are other variables that also predict or describe motion. These include:

- Vectors: Quantities that have both magnitude and direction. Vectors are used to represent physical quantities like force and displacement. For example, a force vector might be described as "ten newtons to the right," where ten newtons is the magnitude and "to the right" is the direction.

- Direction: The line or path along which something is moving, pointing, or aiming. For example, direction tells you where a vector is pointing, such as "north," "upward," or "thirty degrees east of north."

- Magnitude: The size or quantity of something. For example, the magnitude of a velocity vector tells you how fast something is moving, while the magnitude of a force vector tells you how strong the force is.

It is the combination of these elements that creates the conditions in which momentum can be generated and sustained. These elements also provide scientists and laypeople multiple opportunities for observing and measuring momentum—detecting it in the physical world, and exploring how it may appear in the psychological experience for those in the midst of it.

The History of Momentum in Science

It is not our intention that this book become a textbook. However, numerous scientists have examined important elements of the science of momentum over the years and integrating their insights was paramount in our work.

The concept of momentum has been studied for thousands of years. But the modern scientific understanding of momentum began to take shape during the sixteenth and seventeenth centuries with the work of scientists such as Galileo Galilei, Johannes Kepler, and Isaac Newton. Galileo is credited with first describing the concept of inertia, which is the property of matter that resists changes in motion. His experiments with rolling balls down inclined planes demonstrated that the speed of a moving object remained constant as long as no external forces acted upon it.

Kepler's laws of planetary motion, which he developed based on observations of the movements of planets, also contributed to the development of the modern understanding of momentum. His laws describe the relationships between the speed and position of planets as they orbit the sun.

Isaac Newton's laws of motion, which he published in 1687 in his work *Philosophiæ Naturalis Principia Mathematica* (*Mathematical Principles of Natural Philosophy*), represented a significant milestone in the understanding of momentum. Newton's laws state that an object will remain at rest or in uniform motion in a straight line unless acted upon by an external force and that the force acting on an object is proportional to its mass times its acceleration.

These laws provide a framework for understanding the behavior of objects in motion, including the concepts of momentum and kinetic energy.

Generations of scientists since have conducted experiments and made discoveries that have contributed to the refinement of the concept of momentum. Some notable examples include the work of James Joule in the mid-nineteenth century, who demonstrated the relationship between heat and energy, and the experiments of Albert Einstein in the early twentieth century, which led to the development of the theory of relativity.

Modern scientists from various fields of physics continue to study and explore the concept of momentum in specific conditions. For example, Steven Chu studies momentum at the atomic level; Wolfgang Ketterle studies momentum in microscopic systems; and William Phillips, Claude Cohen-Tannoudji, and Eric Cornell all study momentum in atoms at extremely low temperatures. These Nobel laureates are advancing the scientific understanding of momentum in directions Newton and Kepler could never have imagined possible.

Momentum and Its Cousins, Inertia and Success

There are a few concepts related to momentum, and sometimes confused for it: inertia and success. While inertia and momentum are related concepts in physics and in life, they have distinct meanings and applications.

Inertia is the property of matter that resists changes in its state of motion. It is related to Newton's First Law of Motion, which states that an object at rest will remain at rest and an object in motion will continue moving at a constant velocity along a straight line unless acted upon by an external force. Inertia is directly linked to an object's mass—the greater the mass, the greater the inertia.

Inertia is often associated with an object's resistance to changes in its velocity or motion. For example, a heavy object requires more force to set it in motion or to stop it compared to a lighter object with less inertia. Inertia is also responsible for the tendency of moving objects to continue moving in the absence of external forces.

Similarly—at least in terms of the popular concept of momentum—"success" is a related term. Momentum and success are linked, yes—but they are also distinct from each other in a few important ways. Success refers to achieving a goal or desired outcome, often as a result of hard work, talent, skill, or some combination of these factors. Success can be a onetime event, such as winning a championship or securing a major business deal, or it can be an ongoing state, such as a successful career or a thriving business. Momentum, on the other hand, is more the feeling or state of mind that builds over time as a result of a series of successful outcomes or positive events. It is the sense that things are going in a positive direction and that success (or more success) is on the horizon.

One way to think about the difference between momentum and success is to consider an athlete who has won a major championship. The athlete has achieved success, but they may or may not have a sense of momentum. If the athlete feels that their win was a fluke or that they got lucky, they may not have a sense of momentum going into their next competition.

Finally, it's important to consider that momentum is time-limited and fragile. Even a single setback or failure can break the positive feedback loop that generated the momentum, leading to a loss of confidence and energy. This is why momentum is often described as a "fleeting" or "transient" state.

The temporality of momentum is noted by many scientists and practitioners alike. In our interviews, various people noted that momentum isn't (and shouldn't be) endlessly sustainable but rather a force that comes in waves. Visualizing momentum through various

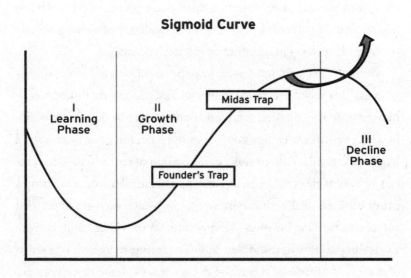

models, Coach Sue Semrau sees momentum as a sigmoid curve, and General Bernie Banks thinks about it as something analogous to how the Yerkes-Dodson curve depicts the relationship between arousal and performance.

In both of these models, successes punctuate, and momentum ebbs and flows.

We recognize momentum as a cycle—it can't and shouldn't be the constant goal. We aren't suggesting that if you get on a roll that it goes forever. The question is—how to make it go five plays longer, five minutes longer, one quarter longer.

Measuring Mo

To measure something, it first must be perceptible. While there's a range of how momentum is perceived, there's no doubt it can be felt. And people sure put their money where their Mo is.

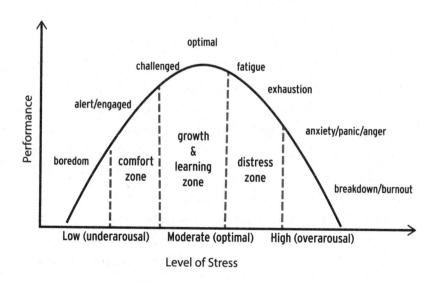

Large-scale data studies have demonstrated that professional gamblers bet more on teams that they perceive as having momentum, and not just by a little bit. One study analyzed a high-frequency dataset of a major bookmaker in German football, and found that bettors stake about 40 percent more on teams that they believe have momentum versus those that just lost a game.

Even though this analysis also found no evidence that perceived momentum mattered on average for match outcomes, and didn't seem to be associated with the bookmaker offering more favorable odds, the perception of momentum nevertheless influenced betting behavior.

Another study, looking at sports betting in the NBA, similarly found the existence of a "momentum effect" in which gamblers incorporate beliefs about momentum into their bets. These studies illustrate that sports bettors trust momentum as a variable that matters to future outcomes but, at the same time, seem to overstate its influence relative to other factors.

Indeed, there's a spectrum of where people place Mo in terms of its relative influence on outcomes—sometimes depending on whether they're on the giving or receiving side of it.

In social psychology, there are various concepts relating to how, or what, people attribute successes or failures to. With attribution bias, people tend to explain others' behavior based on individual characteristics rather than considering external factors. For example—to assume that a person struggling to find employment is lazy rather than to believe that situations in that person's life have left them at a difficult disadvantage. The opposite concept, "self-serving bias," reverses these assumptions. Here a person may attribute their own successes to their personal characteristics or efforts rather than to the environment around them. To keep with the prior analogy, a young person who scores a high-paying job may attribute this hiring to their own competence versus family connections to the company's leadership.

Sometimes, though, Mo can be felt even before an outcome happens—before the winning shot is scored or a battlefield captured. People self-report how they, or full crowds, seem to recognize momentum when it's just about to happen—not just as a retrospective explanation for a success but as a qualitative feeling as it's approaching.

How, then, can Mo be measured?

Finding the Right Indicators and Tools

The issue with momentum isn't an "I'll believe it when I see it" kind of thing. Because people do believe it exists and do believe they've seen it. Rather, the challenge is finding scientific tools that are sensitive enough to measure Mo in social contexts—such as in military, sports, business, or politics.

Unlike in a controlled physics experiment where mass and speed can be precisely measured, momentum in everyday life may lack clear, objective indicators.

While all instances of momentum involve motion, or a surge in progress, not all occurrences of progress are, in fact, momentum. We know that success isn't itself momentum. How much progress or how much success does it take for something to reach a threshold of being momentous? Is it a quantity of progress, or a feeling of it?

Questions like these, where the dependent variable itself is uncertain, can be uncomfortable in hard science, but not impossible. The scientific method requires investigators to disprove a hypothesis that an observed outcome is simply chance. In some studies, the dependent variable (outcome) and independent variables (factors that may influence it) are easy to measure and are highly distinct from one another.

Take, for example, a study on how light travels in different conditions. The null hypothesis could be something like "There's no difference in the speed of light in a vacuum and in water." Data would be collected by objective tools, and the null hypothesis would ultimately be rejected—after tests and retests, it would be shown that light does in fact travel at different speeds in different mediums.

Other questions involve some degree of subjectivity, such as in drug trials on the effectiveness of pain medication. For example, the "null hypothesis" may be that there's no difference in pain relief between drug A and a placebo. In a controlled trial, researchers may find that patients who took drug A and patients given a placebo look about the same, statistically, in terms of self-reported pain levels. In this case, the null hypothesis couldn't be rejected, and any differences in pain levels between treatment and placebo groups may be explained by mere chance.

Finally, there are questions that involve either huge numbers of variables, high levels of subjectivity, or both. That's where studies on momentum in social situations often fall. In a classic social experiment on momentum, researchers are tasked with disproving the assumption that a sustained surge in performance falls within a range that could be explained by chance.

Recently, a study by University of Wisconsin–Milwaukee professor Paul Roebber found evidence that momentum is real in football and can improve a team's chances of winning. His research defined momentum as a consistent change in win probability over at least three successive changes of possession. The results showed momentum streaks occur more often than random chance would predict. Roebber's study identified a physiological basis for momentum called the "winner effect," where success leads to increased testosterone and reduced stress hormones. This provides a biological explanation for how momentum could manifest.

These efforts, largely designed to prove the existence or influence of momentum, are a great starting point. But it's another set of questions that interests us the most: What are the differences between surging teams that win in overtime compared with the surging teams that don't? What separates organizations that are able to maintain momentum between quarters and those that can't? What types of communications between group members maximize cohesion and reduce friction—a top enemy of Mo?

We start with the premise that momentum exists and can be manipulated by intentional types of preparation and organizational structure, and we give the following definition:

> Momentum is a synergistic force that influences the progress, resilience, and focus of a team; and its impact on the mindset of a team—positively or negatively—can be manipulated and extended.

From here, this book explores research to inform leaders and teams about the elements that will amplify their chances of preparing for momentum, seizing the reins of a surge, and carrying it into sustained momentum.

That's what our model offers, and we look forward to going there with you.

3

Overview of the
Momentum Model

The fabled social psychologist Kurt Lewin once said, "There is nothing so practical as a good theory." When leaders leverage rigorous models, frameworks, and theories, they can enhance their probability of generating a successful outcome because they think more holistically about their approach. A recent example of utilizing such an approach is Microsoft under Satya Nadella's stewardship.

Steve Ballmer served as the chief executive officer of Microsoft from 2000 to 2014. During his tenure, the company's revenue grew by 300 percent, and the profit rose by 200 percent. Yet the company's stock price was lower when he departed than when he took over. Why? Investors thought the company was overreliant on legacy products and resistant to championing emerging opportunities (for example, open-source computing and smartphones). Conversely, Apple's stock had risen from $50 to $500 during that same time frame. It was apparent to the Microsoft board that the company needed to generate positive momentum, and Satya Nadella was their choice to make it happen.

Nadella joined Microsoft in 1992 and rose through its ranks, ultimately serving as the executive vice president of the Cloud and Enterprise Group before it was announced on February 4, 2014, that he would become the company's third chief executive officer. In the years since then, Nadella and his team have executed a brilliant strategic pivot that relied on generating positive innovation momentum through the firm while using some noted change frameworks.

A brief examination of Nadella's (and his team's) early years of repositioning the company reveals that they strongly adhered to John Kotter's and Kurt Lewin's celebrated change models and Edgar Schein's cultural change mechanisms. Most importantly, Nadella recognized the need to generate positive momentum and declared shortly after assuming the CEO role that it was time to "rediscover the soul of Microsoft, our reason for being."

Once he assumed the CEO role, Nadella immediately sought to establish a "sense of urgency" while "unfreezing" the organization. He "induced anxiety" by highlighting the changing technology landscape and why it was imperative to compete with cloud-first companies (for example, Google and Amazon). Nadella employed data to show the reality of Microsoft's situation while also emphasizing to the workforce that he was one of them. He undertook all the aforementioned actions in service of shocking people out of their comfort zone.

Two actions were emblematic of Nadella's commitment to building a core group of change leaders. First was his directive to invite the former CEOs and chief technology officers (CTOs) of every company Microsoft had acquired in 2013 to the organization's prized executive retreat (the executive retreat traditionally involved taking the top 150 leaders in the company to a luxurious off-site location for high-level discussions). The summit invitation was noteworthy because many individuals did not possess high enough role responsibility post-acquisition to qualify for attending the conclave. Furthermore, the managers of the invited group fell below the codified invitation qualification level! Nadella was challenging convention and culture in taking this approach. But he was committed to leveraging the different perspectives as a forcing function.

Second was the decision to conduct customer visits to a cross section of the company's accounts by senior leaders together. This edict, too, was unusual. There were many leaders who pushed back on the need to conduct such visits. An undercurrent of the resistance was rooted in the perspective that account leads had a good handle on how to best serve their customers. Thus, there was no need to bring leaders from across the company to conduct visits together. Yet, Nadella held people accountable for following through on his instruction. The ensuing interactions fostered more effective alignment among business units and revealed friction points that could be addressed through cultural modifications.

In the mid-1970s, Bill Gates had established the mission of Microsoft as "a computer on every desk and in every home." The reality in 2014 was that the company had effectively accomplished that mission in developed and industrialized countries. Consequently, the statement was no longer a driver of significant growth and innovation. Nadella understood the need to reimagine and "communicate the company's vision" as part of the effort to reestablish its momentum. Ultimately, Nadella's team landed on "to empower every person and every organization on the planet to achieve more" as the coalescing vision and started sharing it during customer visits and company gatherings.

The ability to unlock dormant organizational potential is highly correlated with "empowering others to act." Prior to Nadella's tenure, software development teams could not share code within the company. He quickly removed that restriction as an act of empowerment. Nadella also encouraged the company's employees to more intentionally explore emerging technologies regardless of their perceived linkage to Windows. He wanted to let great talent figure out how to make great things possible by loosening the restrictions placed on them.

The ability to generate momentum is aided by leveraging short-term wins that demonstrate tangible accomplishments. Nadella reduced some of the organization's anxiety regarding internal competition by eliminating the process that forced managers to designate a small percentage of their team as underperformers. He also moved to create partnerships with longtime competitors in service of expanding the company's product portfolio. Such actions heralded an "it's a new day" mentality that people perceived as positive momentum.

Finally, Nadella has continued to build upon the varied initiatives and sustain the change momentum while also actively modifying the company's culture. He's reorganized the company, tied executive bonuses to talent objectives, and instilled a "learn it all" set of norms. In doing so, the company's market capitalization has grown from approximately $300 billion in 2014 to $3.10 trillion in 2024! The explosion in market capitalization came in no small measure through the reinstallation and sustainment of momentum.

Just as Nadella created a model to make bold changes within Microsoft, we have distilled hundreds of interviews with leaders to create a model for teams and leaders hoping to ride the wave that momentum can provide. In this chapter, we'll share our model and give you a quick understanding of each element.

Why a Model and Not a Formula?

If you've picked up this book, it's likely you've read other texts relating to leadership, business theory, or team building. It's also likely you've seen guides that offer a "recipe for success" or a "blueprint for action" that promise leaders that if they follow a certain script, they can expect a certain result.

Indeed, that's what most formulas promise: You plug your own content in, and those inputs will generate an expected result.

In various fields of study, from mathematics and science to economics and engineering, the terms *formula* and *model* are frequently used. Although these terms might seem interchangeable at first glance—and often are in popular speech—they represent different concepts and serve distinct purposes in the analysis, interpretation, and understanding of complex systems.

Formulas are ubiquitous in science and engineering. In physics, for example, Newton's Second Law of Motion is expressed as $F = ma$ where F represents force, m represents mass, and a represents acceleration. This formula precisely quantifies how much force is needed to accelerate an object of a given mass. Formulas are typically more straightforward, focusing on a single relationship at a time.

In contrast, a model is fundamentally a simplified representation of a real-world system, process, or concept. It is a tool used to explain, predict, or understand how different components of a system interact with one another. Their primary purpose is to help practitioners make sense of complex phenomena by breaking them down into more manageable components.

For instance, in economics, a model might represent the relationship between supply and demand in a market. This model might include various factors such as price, consumer behavior, and production costs, all of which interact in complex ways. By simplifying these relationships into a model, economists can predict how changes in one variable, like a price increase, might affect the overall market.

No model is a perfect representation of reality; instead, it is a useful approximation that helps us navigate and make decisions in the real world.

Models provide the broad framework for understanding complex systems. They aren't plug-and-play like formulas are, and they are by design an overgeneralization that can be applied to multiple conditions.

Our model for momentum is just that.

In the early days of our research, through hundreds of hours of interviews, original surveys, and deep dives into the literature on team dynamics, we noticed a pattern emerging across various fields—whether in business, military operations, politics, or sports. Leaders and strategists in each domain faced similar challenges when it came to optimizing team performance, fostering a positive climate, and achieving their objectives. Despite the apparent differences in context, the underlying principles of effective teamwork and leadership seemed to be strikingly similar.

This observation led us to a question: Could there be a workable model that can be applied across these diverse domains, one that could adapt to teams of different natures, sizes, and structures? The resulting model is both flexible and robust, capable of addressing the unique demands of any context while maintaining a core set of principles that drive success.

But even a great model—one that explains performance in other teams and can drive success for your own—doesn't mean that if you do *a*, *b*, and *c*, you're guaranteed momentum. A good model allows you to start preparing yourself. A great model allows many people to create action.

Formulas are great—for baking, chemists, and predicting the paths of physical objects in space. But formulas have their limits when it comes to human interactions and group dynamics. Rather, we look to models as our guide.

The story we shared about the transformation of Microsoft under Satya Nadella's leadership highlights a process of organizational renewal guided in part by leveraging John P. Kotter's research and famed "8-step change model" from his 1995 management classic, *Leading Change*, and follow-up 2014 book, *Accelerate: Building Strategic Agility for a Faster Moving World*. Just as Kotter's model helped to guide Nadella's actions, it also informed our exploration of generating organizational momentum.

Our model of momentum draws on the flywheel concept in Jim Collins's *Good to Great*; it's a powerful conceptual model for how successful companies achieve sustained growth. Where Kotter's model is more linear—a set of eight steps that generally follow from one to the next—Collins's model is a bit more cyclical or dynamic, representing the cumulative effect of consistent effort and strategic decisions over time, which ultimately leads to a breakthrough.

Kotter's 8 Step Change Model

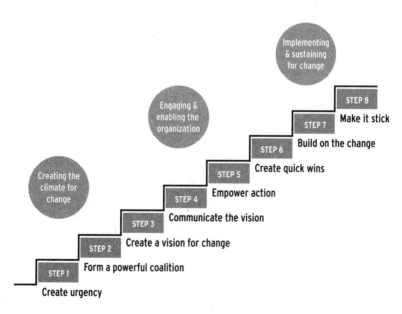

Kotter's model starts with creating a sense of urgency, building a coalition, and forming strategic vision. From there, leadership would enlist a "volunteer army" and enable action by removing barriers to change. Finally, in Kotter's model, short-term wins would be generated and leveraged to sustain acceleration and, ultimately, institute more lasting change.

Collins's "flywheel" includes some similar elements, such as leadership curating a team of disciplined people who engage in disciplined thought and action. His model begins with the building of momentum, which he describes as the force that starts the flywheel spinning. Subsequently, Collins detailed a construct called the "Hedgehog Concept" to help people understand the optimal place to direct organizational energy as part of the flywheel process. The concept seeks to ensure actions are focused on operating at the intersection of three questions: (1) What are you deeply passionate about? (2) What can you be the best in the world at? and (3) What best drives your

The Hedgehog Concept

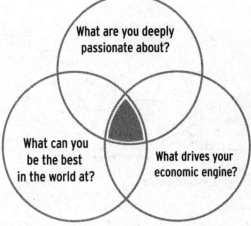

economic or resource engine? Adhering to the Hedgehog Concept generates the energy to move the flywheel. It can require immense effort to get this started, but with consistent effort, you can ultimately reach a "breakthrough point" where the wheel moves more on its own—with its own momentum.

Our model of momentum shares elements of both Kotter's and Collins's ideas: a sequence of events that includes a series of inputs that repeat, feeding progress. In other words, our model is both linear and cyclical, and it could be seen as a precursor or prequel to Collins's flywheel—a model that zooms in on what it takes to get element one—momentum—started.

A Model for Momentum

Just as Jim Collins and John Kotter have provided foundational frameworks in the fields of leadership and organizational change, our

The Flywheel Concept by Jim Collins

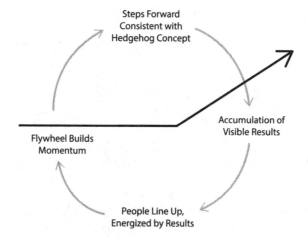

Steps Forward Consistent with Hedgehog Concept

Accumulation of Visible Results

Flywheel Builds Momentum

People Line Up, Energized by Results

research has led to the creation of a comprehensive model for under-standing and generating momentum within teams and organizations. Through extensive interviews, rigorous data analysis, and a thorough review of the existing literature, we have identified nine intercon-nected elements that are crucial for optimizing momentum: leader-ship, culture, recruitment, preparation, spark, leader communications, team climate, belief and mindset, and outcomes and feedback. These elements not only work together to maximize the positive effects of momentum but can also serve as tools for reversing its downturn when an organization finds itself struggling. Each of these factors will be explored in depth in the following chapters, providing you with actionable insights and strategies.

Before diving into the specific chapters, we want to give you a clear overview of how these components interact and reinforce one another. By considering how they show up in your own organization, you can begin to assess where the sparks of momentum may emerge and how you can harness them to drive sustained success. Momentum

Our Model Of Momentum

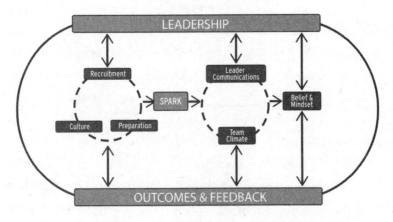

isn't simply about capitalizing on favorable moments—it's about understanding how to prepare for them, actively create them, shape them, and even work against them when things seem to be going against your team.

LEADERSHIP

"A leader takes people where they want to go. A great leader takes people where they don't necessarily want to go but ought to be."

—ROSALYNN CARTER

For the purposes of this model, the focus is on the action leaders take across multiple domains in service of effectively building upon moments. Leadership is a phenomenon examined at the individual, group, and organizational levels of analysis. Countless people have sought to codify the knowledge, skills, and attributes associated with effective leaders.

In the following chapter, you'll hear from renowned leaders we interviewed for this book, including General David Petraeus, sharing both theoretical and tactical tips for structuring leadership in a way that maximizes impact on every other element of this model: Leaders recruit; leaders shape culture; leaders drive preparation and the ability for team members to recognize both the various forms and shapes of spark; leaders communicate with teams to take action when it happens; leaders set the tone for team climate; and leaders foster beliefs and mindsets. Finally, leaders provide and accept feedback from major and passing outcomes, processing these inputs and using them to inform the next actions—the next recruitments, preparations, communications, and more.

CULTURE

"The only thing of real importance that leaders do is to create and manage culture. If you do not manage culture, it manages you, and you may not even be aware of the extent to which this is happening."

—EDGAR SCHEIN

In "The Leader's Guide to Corporate Culture," Boris Groysberg, Jeremiah Lee, Jesse Price, and J. Yo-Jud Cheng characterized culture as "an organization's tacit social order that shapes attitudes and behaviors in a lasting way." Edgar Schein's key article "Issues in Understanding and Changing Culture" defined culture as a "pattern of basic assumptions—invented, discovered, or developed by a given group as it learns to cope with its problems, external adaptation, and internal integration—that has worked well enough to be considered valid and, therefore, to be taught to new members as the correct way to perceive, think, and feel in relation to those problems." Said in the most basic of ways, culture is all about the norms, values, and shared beliefs that guide the behavior of people in a social group.

In the culture chapter, you will take lessons from our interview with Coach Steve Kerr and others to gain insights about what types of organizational norms and behaviors support the generation of positive momentum and reversal of negative momentum. Creating an effective culture is the responsibility of organizational leaders, because culture's proper role is to facilitate an entity's ability to execute its desired strategy in an efficient and effective manner. Therefore, leaders must always examine the question "What is the culture we require in order to do the things we desire?"

RECRUITMENT

For a team to seize momentum, it requires that nearly all the team members are willing to do what is best for the team. Team success must be a higher priority than individual success. A culture of "We" as opposed to "I" is essential in this pursuit.

In the recruitment chapter, you'll be given the opportunity to identify which elements, or qualities in individuals, may maximize an organization's chances to set the stage for momentum to occur or be enhanced. We will discuss the elements of team building across our four pillars, and will conclude with a discussion of interpersonal dynamics and potential assessment tools that can aid in identifying and recruiting "team players" and developing a "momentum culture."

You'll also hear from our original interviews with a handful of leaders in sports, government administration, and business—including renowned basketball coach Sue Semrau, manager and World Series winner David Ross, Veterans Administration leader and CEO Bob McDonald, and FanDuel CEO Amy Howe. While recruitment, culture, and preparation all share space on a wheel, which lacks hierarchy, there's a reason why we place recruitment on the top of the circle.

PREPARATION

Preparation may be the most widely studied and acknowledged input for success: John Wooden, Vince Lombardi, Peter Drucker, Jim Collins, and many others have popularized the deep importance of preparation and practice for success. But in our model, preparation means something more: being prepared not only to perform your role optimally but to spot and react to momentum, to sparks.

Specifically, how does one prepare to seize a moment?

If you're only reacting to momentum once it's happening, you're already at a disadvantage—whether you're on the positive or negative side of the phenomenon. Spotting Mo—and the spark(s) that precedes it—isn't just about predicting game outcomes or enjoying the thrill of those moments. The ability to spot Mo is essential for individuals and teams in order to capitalize on momentum.

Here, you'll read from our conversations with Nvidia cofounder Chris Malachowsky, Coach Buzz Williams, and famed political consultants James Carville and John McLaughlin to explore the elements necessary to prepare for and generate momentum before the surge begins, and lay the groundwork to make yourself receptive to the mental and physical processes triggered by a realization of momentum.

SPARK

"Momentum doesn't exist until you get that first victory. Before that, it's just motivation."

—JOHN MAXWELL

Victories aren't always ultimate wins. In the military context, there are battles, and they may be a long way from determining the outcome of the war. Momentum is not static. Momentum is, by its very definition, movement. Sparks can initiate the movement if the right team has been recruited, they are communicating, and they are prepared.

In this chapter, we continue our conversation with Nvidia's Chris Malachowsky and others to define and flesh out the various forms of spark that exist and that can be leveraged. In every competition there will be moments of opportunity—though sometimes it's a matter of knowing what to look for. An improperly prepared team may miss a spark entirely or fail to react to it. Then the moment is gone. In sports, they call these "sudden change situations." These are events that must be responded to immediately, such as an interception or fumble. In politics, we've all seen squandered opportunities for a candidate to react or respond to events or opponents' foibles. In business, one of the most certain ways to fail to capture a spark is to assign a committee to evaluate an issue rather than taking decisive action.

You'll get a feel for the various shapes, sizes, and feels of spark—and through this, become equipped to spot it . . . and, better yet, to act upon it with your team.

LEADER COMMUNICATIONS

A spark has happened! The catalyst—the opportunity a team has waited for—is at hand. What now? This chapter explores the instrumental role of coaches, CEOs, and other leaders who have prepared their teams for momentum and then must communicate to teams that *this* is the moment. You'll learn from our conversations with General David Petraeus, Blue Cross CEO Pat Geraghty, and prolific tech exec Rohan Chandran about tools that can be developed and deployed to maximize how your teams respond to sparks and leader inputs, and you'll be given a concrete guide for how to navigate dynamics where multiple leaders must communicate in concert.

TEAM CLIMATE

> "Trust comes from intimacy, and the leader has got to build that intimacy, and then you've got to develop these quick wins."

> —BOB MCDONALD

Transference of energy is one of the key properties of creating momentum. It is also the secret to building momentum within a team. But how does this process happen? Here, you'll explore multiple phenomena including imitation, mirroring, and "emotional contagion" between members of an organization or team.

This chapter also incorporates what we've learned from interviews with WD-40 CEO Garry Ridge and neuroscientist Marco Iacoboni on the role of intrateam competition and other related dynamics, and you'll get your hands on practical tips from leaders in diverse fields on ways to strengthen connections between members of a team.

BELIEF AND MINDSET

Beliefs are what individuals and organizations hold to be true. Mindsets are ways of thinking or relating to these shared beliefs. At the very least, belief and mindset are complementary concepts, but when it comes to manipulating momentum, our model suggests that both are essential. Members of a team can believe that momentum is real. But if they don't share a common mindset or ethos of how to approach momentum, opportunities will quickly be lost.

This chapter, with insights from our discussions with basketball coach Cori Close, researcher John Hollenbeck, and neuroscientist Jaime Pineda, dives deep into how the mind processes information and, in turn, shapes behavior, performance, and outcomes. Through scientific evidence and anecdotal exploration, you'll examine how shared belief systems, and shared mindsets, can be developed and fine-tuned to perceive signals of momentum and enhance a team's ability to cohesively respond.

OUTCOMES AND FEEDBACK

An essential factor in generating or maintaining Mo relates to feedback. Feedback is a widely studied topic in psychological research, and it is among the most relatable concepts for people when thinking about their own life experiences. When it comes to momentum, this body of literature has significant application. You'll be given broad context for understanding how feedback works in various settings, and more specifically, how positive feedback fuels the process of momentum.

Through our interview with Blue Angels commander Alexander Armatas and a deep review of the feedback science, you'll learn how to observe feedback in your own organizations, and how to create new channels for receiving and responding to feedback in ways that can generate and sustain team momentum.

4

Leadership

Where momentum may feel easy to experience but surprisingly difficult to define, leadership may suffer from the opposite affliction: There's just so much written about it. There are more than forty thousand books on Goodreads alone in the leadership category and many more on Amazon that touch on this topic. There are books on classical management theories and books on contemporary explorations of leadership in digital and diverse environments. And then there are the academic journals. They range from broad in their orientation—*Leadership* by Sage, for example, which publishes peer-reviewed research on leadership—to highly niche, like *Educational Leadership, Women in Leadership, Journal of Nonprofit Management and Leadership,* and *International Journal of Leadership Studies,* to name a few. A search of the Florida State University unified library system shows a total of 256 journals that relate to leadership; 620,001 academic articles; 181,273 newspaper articles; 176,339 magazine articles; 112,344 dissertations; and 103,836 book chapters. That doesn't count thousands of government documents, conference proceedings, and more—all of that to say, there's quite a lot to say about leadership.

A walk back through the history of definitions of leadership brings us to Ralph Stogdill in 1950, who described leadership as the process of influencing the activities of a group toward achievement—a definition that emphasizes the relational and goal-oriented aspects of this trait. This was followed by James MacGregor Burns, in 1978, whose theory of transformational and transactional leadership advanced the idea that transformational leaders inspire and motivate followers to achieve higher levels of performance and moral development, while transactional leaders focus on exchange and rewards to manage their teams. This distinction had a profound impact on subsequent leadership research, leading to the development of the Multifactor Leadership Questionnaire by Bernard Bass and Bruce Avolio (1995), which operationalizes these constructs.

Burns's concept of transformational versus transactional leadership also inspired the work of Peter G. Northouse, whose 2018 seminal text, *Leadership: Theory and Practice*, makes clear that leadership is not a static trait or characteristic but rather an interaction between the leader and the group members.

Northouse's perspective is that leadership is contextual and can vary depending on the situation and the people involved. Northouse provides two major groupings of leadership definitions: trait and process. Trait theories of leadership seek to identify the innate qualities and characteristics that allow someone to successfully exercise leadership. Researchers have sought to glean what personality, physical, and intelligence factors account for leader effectiveness. Most importantly, trait theories focus solely on the leader and do not examine the follower.

Process theories of leadership, on the other hand, emanate from the perspective that leadership is an event. Therefore, effective leadership results from the quality of interaction between the leader and the follower. Process theories suggest that leadership is a process accessible to everyone. We can best examine momentum when we use a process definition of leadership.

It is important to note that sustained effective leadership requires the presence of a high degree of trust by leaders *and* followers. So, our employment of leadership as a momentum driver incorporates an

The Trust Equation

$$\frac{\text{Credibility} + \text{Reliability} + \text{Emotional Safety (Intimacy)}}{\text{Self-Orientation}} = \text{Trustworthiness}$$

understanding of trust's importance. The "Trust Equation" by David Maister, Charles Green, and Robert Galford is a model that highlights four key components of trustworthiness (credibility, reliability, intimacy, and self-orientation).

Credibility relates to the confidence others have in our knowledge, skills, and track record. It's built through demonstrating our competence and sharing relevant experiences. Trust is difficult to establish if people perceive leaders as unqualified or too inexperienced.

Reliability is about meeting expectations and consistently honoring commitments. It is important to keep one's word and deliver on promises. Leaders that demonstrate reliability foster a sense of trust and confidence in their abilities.

By emotional safety (intimacy), we do not mean to imply that we need to possess a deep personal relationship with someone. Building intimacy creates understanding, familiarity, and security. It leverages empathy, active listening, and a genuine interest in the other person's interests.

Self-orientation examines the extent to which a leader (or leaders) prioritize their own interests over those of others. The more self-oriented leaders are, the less trustworthy they'll appear. Demonstrating a genuine concern for the best interests of others is important.

Northouse also offers us perhaps the most intuitive definition of leadership—one that we, in this book, and many others can use as a starting point for leadership in action: "a process whereby an individual influences a group of individuals to achieve a common goal."

This is why leadership isn't a single component in our model, or even on one of our model's wheels. Rather, it's a primary driver of momentum, an influence that touches nearly every other input, pretty much continually. The preeminence of leadership in this model of momentum is backed up not only by academic research but by the perceptions of thousands of laypeople. In some of our surveys of the general public, we asked how much various factors influence the likelihood of a team experiencing momentum. From a list of nine factors, including many described in our model, "leadership" and "communication from leaders" shake out as the top two most influential.

So, from all of this literature, what makes for a good leader?

For that, we turn to our friend and contributor James Collins, whose 2001 book, *Good to Great: Why Some Companies Make the Leap... and Others Don't*, has become a staple in business circles across sectors. Several large-scale data studies have explored the impact of leadership on organizational performance, and the research in *Good to Great* earned its perennial place on top leadership reading lists ever since.

Over five years, Collins sought to identify the factors that enable good companies to transform into great ones, and examined companies that made such a leap and sustained that performance for at least fifteen years. The research team analyzed 1,435 Fortune 500 companies over a forty-year period, eventually narrowing its focus to eleven companies. Collins found seven conditions that really set these companies apart, and no surprise, leadership was at the top of the list. A Level 5 leader, to Collins, embodies a unique blend of personal humility and professional will. They are often modest and reserved but have an intense determination to do whatever it takes to make the company successful. Importantly, these Level 5 leaders focus more on the success of the organization than on personal recognition.

Outside of business, academic research, and theory—what does "leading for Mo" look like?

A point scored in sports is clear—more baskets made or yards run. A point in politics is clear—an edge up in a poll or more ballots cast on election day. And a point in business is clear—more customers converted or a spike in the value of a stock. But in the military, a point gained or lost may very well be a human life. The stakes are different, weightier—and yet, somehow, often less clear and more complex. Perhaps this is because the scope is larger too. A sports team may have a handful or a few dozen teammates and a few dozen competitors. A political candidate may have a handful of folks to defeat in a primary or a few dozen committee members to persuade on a vote. Businesses can have anywhere from a few employees to many thousand, but the universe of that company is defined, and competitors are generally known and limited. Military conflicts are many orders of magnitude larger, as are the variety of environmental, social, and political factors that can influence outcomes. Add in the fact that, unlike a ninety-minute sports match, a campaign cycle in politics, or an end-of-quarter statement in business, military engagements aren't mutually scheduled. The end can come down to a decision, not a decisive win, and the scoreboard may take years, if not generations, to fully assess.

While these variables may make it difficult to apply lessons from other sectors to the military, it also means that lessons learned in the military context are particularly valuable to those in other fields. If a process works in the high-stakes, high-complexity military context, its application may prove quite powerful elsewhere.

What can civilian leaders learn from military leaders who prepare for, drive, and implement game-changing, momentum-changing decisions? What does momentum look like, and mean, when the unit of measure is human life or shifts in power between nations? How can organizations leverage lessons learned on battlefields to improve their own agility, preparations, and responses to challenge?

Educating leaders outside of the military context was not what General David Petraeus had top of mind in 2007 when he was called upon by President George W. Bush to pick up the pieces of the US engagement in Iraq. By the time he assumed command of the Multi-National Force in Iraq (MNF-I), the situation was dire, and his coalition was losing. It had devolved into spiraling chaos, rampant sectarian violence, and a pervasive sense of hopelessness.

The palpable negative momentum on the ground was only compounded by eroding public support at home. Americans were increasingly skeptical and frustrated by the war's toll, measured in US casualties, billions in spending on military efforts, and a lack of progress in the goal to establish democracy and stability in the region.

Petraeus faced, then, not only the daunting task of turning around an ineffective military strategy in Iraq but also of winning back public support for the effort itself. It didn't look likely.

• • •

When we met with David Petraeus, in the summer of 2023, when we asked the retired general to put himself back in that very moment, it seemed easy. It was as if no time had passed. Even his words often came in the present tense, as though the realness of what he and his team faced in Iraq in February 2007 was still happening, fresh, in that very moment.

"We're trying to break a cycle of violence, which is getting worse and worse. It's spiraling, the country is spiraling downward, and we have to reverse that," he said.

Though no matter how many times Petraeus said the word *we*—then and now—at that moment, the weight of success or failure in the eyes of the world was squarely and almost singularly on his shoulders alone.

Bush was frustrated by the intensifying disarray in Iraq and the risks this posed not only to human life but to his own legacy, and he was sold on the promise of a "new way forward" with Petraeus at the helm. And the president said so, again and again, to the American public. According to one report, Bush mentioned Petraeus's name more than 150 times in speeches and press conferences in the first six months of Petraeus's command.

Petraeus, for his part, urged patience and trust. The challenge would be monumental, but the general was armed with a strategic approach that he believed, if maintained, would prove transformational. He became the public face of the counterinsurgency, communicating directly with the American people and his soldiers alike to an extent never seen before. Fortunately, Petraeus was highly trusted by soldiers and politicians alike, and he leveraged this trust to create strategic patience.

Petraeus's previous experiences had bestowed a high "trust equation" quotient upon him. Most importantly, he was viewed as very competent due to his academic pedigree and intellectual understanding of counterinsurgency. For example, Petraeus had overseen (along with Marine Lieutenant General James F. Amos) the Army's creation of Field Manual 3-4 *Counterinsurgency* in a previous assignment. Furthermore, he had successfully led the 101st Airborne Division in Mosul, Iraq, leveraging nation-building and counterinsurgency doctrine. Petraeus's competence, track record in previous high-visibility command assignments, and clear understanding of the national command authority's interests all contributed to his level of trust and gravitas.

Usually, the person appointed by politicians to PR a problem puts at least some lipstick on the pig. But Petraeus did the opposite. "This is a period in which it gets harder before it gets easier," Petraeus told the *Washington Post* in May 2007. Petraeus wasn't wrong. The first many months of his lead were, in the West Point graduate's own words, "excruciating." Bombings increased, as did their death tolls. More than fifty people died each day in the violence in Baghdad alone. Chemical weapons such as chlorine gas were used for the first time, detonating in three cities. There was an average of one car bombing every day during that time. Calls were rising for the US to withdraw from Iraq.

And then something shifted. That shift was the "surge."

On February 10, 2007, Petraeus gave his first speech in command of the MNF-I. It was his third tour and twenty-eighth month in Iraq. But what he said that day presented a total reversal of everything he'd seen so far. His recollection to us of that moment was once again as sharp as though he'd held that microphone just minutes before.

"You take command, you pass the colors to the sergeant major, you go to the podium, and I said, 'We're going to live with the people to secure them because that is the only way we can do that,'" Petraeus recollected. "But that was the exact opposite of what we'd been doing. Prior to that, we'd been pulling out of the neighborhoods, consolidating on big bases, and handing off security responsibilities to the Iraqi security forces, who could no longer handle the level of violence because it had gotten so bad."

To his troops, Petraeus had just communicated the "population-centric" strategy in which they were expected to deeply integrate into Iraqi communities.

It was, in Petraeus's words, a "180-degree difference" between what they'd been doing before and what they embarked on. "It doesn't get any bigger than that," he reflected, noting how hyperaware he had been of the skepticism surrounding his new strategic direction. Congress was particularly skeptical. During Petraeus's confirmation hearing, he was required to agree that he'd come back at the six-month mark to lay out the results. And that's just about how long it took for many to begin seeing the impacts of the surge.

Petraeus promised he would be "first with the truth" in relaying progress—that he would "beat the bad guys to the headline, but only with what is actually known to be the truth, to be accurate." There would be no lipstick on the pig.

But progress did come.

The shift in strategy was popularly referred to as "Clear, Hold, Build"—in which the US would first clear an area of insurgents and secure it, then maintain a persistent presence to hold the area, and finally, devote resources to the rebuilding of infrastructure, essential services, and local governance.

All of these steps, however, required a significant shift in the US approach to Iraq, beginning with a substantial increase in US troops. About thirty thousand more troops were deployed, particularly in Baghdad and Anbar Province. The goal was to saturate these areas with troops—to create a visible presence within communities, to protect the population, to engage with local leaders, and to ultimately win the trust of the Iraqi people.

Saturating these cities and neighborhoods was no small task. Petraeus established combat outposts and patrol bases everywhere he could, focusing the most attention on those areas that were most central to the violence. They walled each off to control the movement of personnel and utilized everything one could imagine at that time—biometric ID cards, explosive-sniffing dogs, X-rays, and more.

The less violence in neighborhoods, the more trust was built. The US and allies would rebuild medical clinics, markets, and the electrical grid, with each action reinforcing a trend of spiraling upward rather than downward.

A central feature of this engagement was for American forces to secure the cooperation of local Sunni tribal leaders who would in turn help fight against Al-Qaeda and other extremist groups. In some instances, this turned former insurgents into allies and involved the rehabilitation of individuals who otherwise were at risk of being terrorists. Petraeus's team would evaluate Iraqi detainees, identify the most extreme members of them, move them to separate, maximum security facilities, and then work with the rest to convince them to rehabilitate. Petraeus knew that, though it would take significant effort to enhance the training and capabilities of Iraqi security forces, ultimately, this would pave the way for the transition of security responsibilities to Iraqi authorities. While the previous approach had also aimed for Iraqi self-reliance, it was unsuccessful. It took the infusion of a significantly greater US presence in Iraq to prepare their people for sovereignty.

More troops on the ground means more troops to lead. And how Petraeus approached that is where leaders in all sectors can take some notes.

. . .

David Petraeus was generous with us in his time and attention. We were far from the first interviewers, students, or friends to ask him how he turned things around in Iraq. It would have been reasonable for a person of his stature to rehash the past with complacent repetition or to reply with a tired "asked and answered." Far from it, Petraeus relived with and for us the elements of his strategy in Iraq—specifically rethought from the perspective of momentum.

When many leaders come to the same conclusion, independently, it's worth a deeper look. Indeed, General Petraeus's "Four Tasks of Strategic Leaders" aligns remarkably well within our Momentum Model. In these, he shares the elements that strategic leaders should focus on, including many that are familiar to our model: leadership, communications, and feedback in particular.

- **Get the Big Ideas Right:** At the heart of any successful strategy is the formulation of the "right big ideas." Petraeus emphasizes the importance of grounding these ideas in reality and keeping them fresh. "This is the basis for what will become momentum," Petraeus said, emphasizing that by far this first task is the hardest. "If you don't get these right, I don't care how good you are. All the other tasks, you can be the most brilliant, charismatic, compelling communicator, you can set the greatest example, provide inspiration, energy, oversight, all the rest of that, and even have a good plan for how you refine the big ideas. But if you don't get the big ideas right up front, and frankly, if you don't keep them current, if you don't keep them refreshed and renewed and adapted and refined—the rest of it doesn't matter."

Clarity of objective and purpose is central, and it enables the ability to measure outcomes against intended results. Andy Grove, the former CEO of Intel, used an OKR framework (Objectives and Key Results) to highlight the need to have clarity regarding what an organization is intent on achieving.

- **Communicate the Big Ideas; No Spin:** Once the right big ideas are established, effective communication is paramount. Petraeus understood that buy-in from all stakeholders, including the Iraqi people, was essential. He noted, "Everyone has to understand what it is we're trying to do, why we are going about it in that way" and that "we want to get as much agreement and support as we possibly can." His insistence on transparent, fact-based communication was pivotal in maintaining the credibility of his approach. This meant, at first, communicating failures as well as successes. While communicating good news is easier than bad, "you have to communicate the truth," Petraeus insists. "Don't try to spin, because if you spin, you erode the reputation of the organization, of the leader, and then your communication efforts are at risk, and then, they are typically not as effective." Petraeus's tactic with communicating the truth didn't always sit well with some on his side. One mentor of Petraeus came to him, worried about what he described as a "public relations problem" for the general. Petraeus's response was incisive: "Sir, this is not a public relations problem. This is a reality problem. And once the reality truly does measurably change for the better, our communications challenge will be much less, and ultimately it will go away."

- **Lead Implementation and Train for Excellence:** Successful leadership is not confined to formulating ideas and communicating them. It extends to overseeing their implementation. To Petraeus, this means leaders "being the example, the energy, the inspiration ... tracking the great people, keep developing them, and allowing those not measuring up to move on to something else." Petraeus exemplified this by providing hands-on guidance to his team, tracking metrics rigorously, and adapting strategies when needed. "There were events that we did several times a week, to walk a patrol with a unit, somewhere in Iraq, at least twice a week," he said. "So I can actually see it for myself on the ground, which had the added credibility, frankly, of sharing a little bit of risk and degree of hardship with those soldiers who were endeavoring to secure and serve the Iraqi people together with our Iraqi security forces partners."

    In other words, Petraeus didn't expect just his troops to integrate with the Iraqi people; he himself did so too. This contributed to Petraeus's personal rapport with his people as well as his ability to more meaningfully understand their strategic position and track and adjust course as needed.

    But for every successful implementation, adequate training must come first. In the military, there's a structured and institutionalized approach to professional development. "It's not optional," Petraeus explained of the mandatory training that military personnel at all levels undergo, including basic training, specialized training, advanced courses, and impressive, sequential, professionalism programs. Petraeus recognizes that few other government or civilian organizations can match what the military requires of its people as far as training, and that smaller organizations particularly struggle to allocate resources for it. While Petraeus lauds the benefits of formal study to developing leaders, he recognizes this may not be possible for all organizations to provide. "You can make up for this lack of formal study by very extensive self-study," he said, "by reading about others who have gone before you and your profession, others generally, and in any major leadership positions—you know, biographies, histories, and so forth."

Research supports this idea. For example, David Moynihan, Sanjay Pandey, and Bradley Wright concluded that when leaders clearly articulate behavior expectations in terms of both organizational and individual employee practices and insist on high levels of performance in order to achieve organizational goals that clearly communicate high but reasonable performance expectations, there's a measurable increase in employees' understanding and confidence in their work.

- **Collect Data and Refine Through Feedback:** This leads to the final task, which to Petraeus is too often overlooked: refining the big ideas. Petraeus explained this task as the process of "sometimes adding new big ideas, sometimes discarding some, sometimes modifying or adapting. . . . And then you do it again and again and again." This ongoing process of refinement ensured that the strategy remained agile and responsive to changing circumstances. How did Petraeus refine? Through the careful monitoring of objective, key indicators like high-visibility attacks, sectarian violence, and civilian casualties due to this violence. By relentlessly focusing on these metrics and adapting strategies accordingly, he started to see signs of progress. "For momentum to be meaningful," Petraeus said, "it has to be real, it has to be fact based, it has to be, again, shown through objective, rigorous metrics."

The Army's *Doctrine Publication 3-0, Operations* articulates the concept of seizing, retaining, and exploiting the operational initiative, which is the military's focus of gaining momentum. Part of the concept highlights how "effective information management to process information quickly is essential for staying inside the enemy's decision-making cycle. Combined with effective planning, information management helps commanders anticipate enemy actions and develop branches, sequels, or adjustments."

Petraeus recognized that military efforts alone would not bring lasting stability to Iraq. He worked to facilitate political reconciliation among Iraq's various sectarian and ethnic groups, particularly between Shia and Sunni militias. And, through all of this, he made good on his promise of unprecedented transparency in communications to world audiences.

"By the six-month mark, our casualties were now coming down very significantly. Iraqi casualties were down. But the major indicators of the success, the growing momentum of this campaign, were really quite clear. And those, again, were overall attack numbers, the sectarian violence numbers," Petraeus said. He brought in data experts from various intelligence agencies to support the collection of metrics, to challenge the data collected, and to resolve discrepancies. Violence had decreased more than 90 percent. It began to look not just possible but probable that Iraqis would be able to achieve self-governance.

Petraeus led the MNF-I for nineteen months. He arrived at circumstances few thought would, or could, get much better. To most

Americans, the engagement in Iraq was "another Vietnam" at best, and to Iraqis, civil war appeared inescapable. Petraeus was asked to "rescue a failing war," but even though he was known as "the most competitive man on the planet," few thought he could make it happen. But he did. Petraeus left an Iraq that was on its way to self-reliance and self-governance.

Petraeus's four tasks of strategic leaders are no doubt critical and highly relevant both in the military context and across sectors. When it comes to the leader's role in momentum, a few other lessons can be drawn from the great general's approach. We hope Petraeus will indulge our adding of these final two points to his model—lessons we've drawn from his accounts that leaders should take specific note of when developing their approaches to leading Mo.

Empower Your "Field Commanders"

Give individuals enhanced authority to make tactical decisions based on their understanding of local conditions. This allows for greater flexibility and adaptability—all the while maintaining rigorous oversight of outcomes and metrics. Petraeus was not just on the sidelines, although oftentimes leaders have no choice but to remain there. Petraeus himself would routinely accompany troops on patrols to experience firsthand what they were seeing—but no leader can be on every "field" at every time.

These observations helped Petraeus provide field commanders with clear, concise documents to outline the overall mission, the desired end state, and their collective intent, or purpose—and then he'd get out of their way. This is really important. Providing such a clear "leader's intent" (that is, purpose, key tasks, end state) can facilitate the ability to establish and accelerate momentum because subordinate leaders can make decisions in real time to advance achievement of the intent. As they devise plans (the how) to achieve the intent, they can keep building on successes in order to get closer to the objective end state.

A clear leader's intent provides direction and can be used to foster alignment (two of the three elements associated with the Center for Creative Leadership's Leadership Model). Petraeus expected his subordinate commanders to align their actions with this intent, while providing them flexibility to adapt to rapidly changing situations. This type of delegation extended to decisions on resource allocation, troop movements, and engagement with local leaders. Field commanders were encouraged to pursue creative solutions and to share best practices with one another.

Stack Small Wins, and Make Sure Your Team Members Take Note of Them

Perhaps the biggest takeaway from General Petraeus is how momentum—the spark for it and the outcome alike—is born from stacking small wins. In other words, to Petraeus, momentum in Iraq was not a result of one grand event but a culmination of small wins. Reflecting on the building of this shift, Petraeus noted, "It was many small wins, many indicators of progress." These wins weren't isolated incidents but part of a larger trend that was gradually shifting the negative momentum toward a more positive trajectory.

The effect was cumulative.

"Once the people start to believe in your strategy, once your troops start to believe, and once Congress starts to understand it and see that it can actually achieve results, all of a sudden, the problems in getting appropriations and authorizations are much reduced. The resistance, which was considerable at the beginning, goes away," he explained.

In other words, small wins are impactful not only for the ground they gain but also for the resistance they reduce. It's not enough, though, just to have the wins on some hidden tally sheet. The power of these small wins derives from team members knowing they happened—observing, feeling, and believing in them.

In Iraq, Petraeus came in facing resistance from all sides, not the least of which was from members of his country's own team. But surely, through preparing for momentum, seizing the wins when they came, and adjusting through extraordinary attention to feedback, resistance lessened, and momentum was reversed in his—and all of our—favor.

LEADER ACTIONS

Peter G. Northouse's *Leadership: Theory and Practice* (2018) highlighted the prominence of four elements in varied conceptions of leadership: Leadership is a process, leadership involves influence, leadership occurs in groups, and leadership involves common goals. Consequently, the actions leaders should take to foster momentum must positively affect the aforementioned elements.

ACTION 1:
Ensure your team possesses a clear understanding of its purpose and mission.

The ability to advance common goals starts with ensuring shared understanding. There are numerous examples of individuals and teams that lacked a clear understanding of what they were truly meant to accomplish. Some team members might place self-interest above those of the collective. Therefore, a leader must set clear expectations in order to align the team's actions.

ACTION 2:
Enhance trust to amplify influence.

The ability to lead effectively is amplified when a high degree of trust exists. Maister, Green, and Galford's "Trust Equation" highlighted four elements: credibility, reliability, intimacy, and self-orientation (perceived interest alignment). When leaders are asking others to lean into behaviors that might generate some degree of anxiety, followers will undoubtedly conduct a trust assessment before electing to honor the leader's request(s).

ACTION 3:
Model the desired behavior.

Jim Kouzes and Barry Posner's work *The Leadership Challenge* identified five exemplary practices of leadership. "Model the Way" was a practice concerning leaders' "establishment of principles concerning the way people (constituents, peers, colleagues, and customers alike) should be treated and the way they should pursue goals. Leaders create standards of excellence and set an example for others to follow."

The psychology field of behaviorism is based on the idea that all behaviors are learned through conditioning, which is a process of reinforcement and punishment. When leaders model the behavior they expect from others and hold them accountable for embracing those norms through operant conditioning, (a type of learning where behaviors are modified by associating them with consequences), they can set examples of what right looks like when seeking to create momentum.

5

Culture

When Joe Lacob and Peter Guber purchased the Golden State Warriors in July 2010, the $450 million price tag was the second highest in NBA history. One would have thought they were purchasing a team with an extraordinary recent record. Not so.

The Warriors were underwater and had been for many years—with more than double the number of losses (56) as wins (26) in their most recent season—a 31.7 percent winning percentage. Rookie Steph Curry, brought aboard as the seventh overall pick in the draft, was a bright spot in an otherwise dismal season, but overall team performance was hampered by poor defense and a lack of depth. The team struggled to compete in a strong Western Conference, finishing well out of playoff contention. The new owners—a venture capitalist and media exec—knew change was needed. After trying and failing to see the results they wanted with other coaching staff, they brought on Steve Kerr in early 2014 to lead in yet another move questioned by many. After all, Kerr had a great playing career to boast of but no coaching experience of his own.

Kerr's first move as head coach was to assess the existing culture of the Warriors. He found a team with potential but lacking a cohesive culture that emphasized teamwork and innovation. Rather, the culture was individualistic, focusing on the talents of key players rather than fostering a collective identity. Kerr knew that had to change.

Kerr aligned the team's strategies and practices with the desired cultural changes. He introduced a system that emphasized ball movement, unselfish play, a fast-paced style, and something else that isn't on the list of most managers: joy. "It's meant to be fun," Kerr would tell his players. He established a set of four core values: joy, competition, compassion, and mindfulness, and of these, Kerr said, joy is "perhaps the easiest to understand, recognize, and impart."

There are plenty of road maps on coaching strategy but very few—if any—on coaching joy. To Kerr, however, that was the easy part. He'd play music during practice, a deviation from what he described as a "drill sergeant mentality" held by many other coaches, and he noticed quickly how the music would help the players feel "loose and energized." And second, Kerr would promote joy through humor. "This is most noticeable in our daily video sessions, when we review game film. The team has a great video editor, and my staff and I often have him splice in some humor, whether from movies, the sports media, or other sources. Sometimes it's just random funny stuff, but a lot of times it's something relevant to our team—maybe something mildly embarrassing someone did or said—intended to get us laughing about ourselves and each other."

For compassion, Kerr knew that genuine care toward one another can't be manufactured—but he certainly saw opportunities to build it. He'd invite parents, children, and the people closest to players to join the team on the road for group dinners and on the team plane. He wanted players to recognize in one another their struggles, vulnerabilities, and shared human experiences. And some of the techniques Kerr would use to foster compassion were amplified by his focus on mindfulness too: yoga, breathing exercises, and meditation. He'd bring in outside talent to lead these sessions, all with the goal to foster connectedness and the ability to enter "the zone."

This approach required buy-in from all players, not just the stars, to work together and prioritize team success over individual achievements. To communicate the desired culture, Kerr consistently reinforced the principles of teamwork, collaboration, and joy in playing the game. He used team meetings, practice sessions, and one-on-one conversations to emphasize these values. Kerr also encouraged open communication and input from players, fostering a sense of ownership and involvement in the cultural shift.

Kerr led by example, embodying the new cultural values. He demonstrated a collaborative and inclusive leadership style, valuing contributions from all team members and staff. Kerr's approachability and willingness to listen set a standard for the entire organization. Perhaps more importantly, he reinforced the new culture by recognizing and rewarding behaviors that aligned with the team's values. Players who demonstrated unselfish play, strong work ethic, and teamwork were celebrated. The organization also invested in player development and wellness programs, further supporting the cultural emphasis on holistic success.

Kerr understood that cultural change is a gradual process. He was patient and persistent, continuously reinforcing the new cultural norms and values over multiple seasons. The evolution of the Warriors' culture involved ongoing adjustments and refinements to maintain alignment with the desired values. And the results were remarkable.

Kerr's first season with the Warriors saw a 67–15 record. They rated first in the NBA on defense and second on offense. And by the 2015–16 season, the Warriors had the best regular-season record in NBA history: 73–9, surpassing the 1995–96 Chicago Bulls' 72-win season and setting a record maintained to the day of this writing. The Warriors went on to win the 2016–17 and 2017–18 championships.

Despite the overwhelmingly positive reaction, some critics were skeptical about the sustainability of the Warriors' transformation and playing style, particularly their heavy reliance on three-point shooting. But continued success and championships silenced most doubters. Sustainable it has been.

The Golden State Warriors topped the *Forbes* annual valuations list for NBA teams for the first time in their history in 2022 and then topped the list again in 2023 with a value of $7.7 billion. Their 2022–23 season generated $765 million in revenue, nearly 50 percent more than any other NBA team. It seems that player joy translates to fan joy too. The cultural transformation under Kerr's leadership led to remarkable outcomes for both the development and success of individual players and the team's performance as a whole. His approach not only led to championships but also revolutionized the style of play in the NBA, making the Warriors one of the most successful and influential teams of the modern era.

Jensen Huang and Steve Kerr may not be anything like each other in disposition, and they may never have read something written by Edgar Schein, the organizational psychologist who developed influential theories on organizational culture and its management. But Huang's transformation of Nvidia and Kerr's transformation of the Golden State Warriors closely mirror each other, and both reflect the principles of Schein's theory in practice.

Indeed, the influence of Schein's scholarship on management theory and practice is so pervasive it may be difficult to separate what has been consciously inspired by his work and what came organically or intuitively to various leaders across sectors. Schein's model has greatly contributed to understanding how culture influences organizational dynamics and performance.

To Schein, the core function of leadership is managing culture. To Huang, "great ideas can come from anyone, anywhere. It's about creating an environment where those ideas can flourish." To Kerr, culture management is "the only thing of real importance that leaders do."

So, what is culture?

In *Organizational Culture and Leadership*, Edgar Schein defines *culture* as "the deeper level of basic assumptions and beliefs that are shared by members of an organization, that operate unconsciously and define in a basic 'taken for granted' fashion an organization's view of itself and its environment" (5th ed., 2016). In simpler terms, Schein suggests that an organization's culture is shaped early on by its founders and leaders. Their actions and beliefs set the tone, shaping culture through shared experiences, leading by example, and reinforcing behaviors that align with their values. In other words, leaders create culture by offering opportunities for group members to connect through things like rituals, stories, and traditions. And they serve as role models, using their behavior to set the standard for everyone else, while rewarding and reinforcing the actions they want to see more of.

Schein identifies three distinct levels of organizational culture, each representing varying degrees of visibility and awareness:

- *Artifacts:* These are the visible and tangible elements of culture, such as architecture, office layout, dress code, and formal processes. Artifacts are easy to observe but difficult to interpret accurately without understanding the deeper levels of culture.

- *Espoused Values:* These are the stated values and norms that an organization explicitly endorses. They include mission statements, codes of ethics, and articulated beliefs. Espoused values provide insights into the organization's desired culture but may not always reflect actual behavior.

- *Underlying Assumptions:* These are the unconscious, taken-for-granted beliefs, perceptions, thoughts, and feelings that truly drive behavior within the organization. Underlying assumptions are deeply embedded and hard to change, but they form the essence of the culture.

Schein once said that "culture is not a surface phenomenon; it is our very core." What this really means is that leaders must play an active role in shaping the cultural norms needed to execute strategy

Edgar Schein's Organization Culture Model

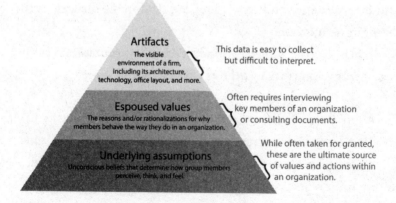

Artifacts
The visible environment of a firm, including its architecture, technology, office layout, and more.

This data is easy to collect but difficult to interpret.

Espoused values
The reasons and/or rationalizations for why members behave the way they do in an organization.

Often requires interviewing key members of an organization or consulting documents.

Underlying assumptions
Unconscious beliefs that determine how group members perceive, think, and feel.

While often taken for granted, these are the ultimate source of values and actions within an organization.

efficiently and effectively. On top of that, they have to build a culture that allows the organization to quickly adapt to opportunities or handle challenges when they come up.

Schein also points out that culture is essential for helping an organization adapt to the world around it and maintain strong internal alignment. It's the guidebook that tells people how to deal with challenges, make decisions, and work together smoothly. Externally, culture shapes how a company interacts with customers, competitors, and regulators. It affects the strategies, goals, and practices that help the company succeed in its environment. Internally, it creates cohesion by establishing shared language, norms, and values. Simply put, culture helps people understand their roles, resolve conflicts, and collaborate more effectively.

If you're trying to build momentum, embedding cultural norms that promote agility can be a game changer. A five-year study of

Factors That Drive Agility

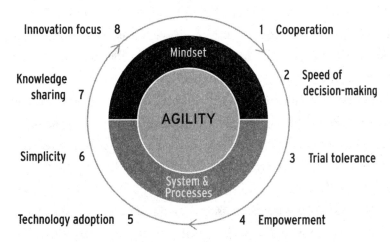

workers in US and European companies, conducted by Gallup, identified eight factors that influence how quickly an organization can respond to business needs—these are what Gallup called the "Agile 8."

Gallup's research also highlighted how central managers are in shaping the employee experience. A key takeaway from a 2018 Gallup article was that "only half of employees globally know what's expected of them at work." It's tough to respond quickly when employees don't know what their responsibilities are. The article also pointed out several key leadership behaviors that support the Agile 8 cultural norms, such as engaging the workforce, proactively managing performance, coaching and developing team members, and collaborating well with other managers. These behaviors are closely aligned with the elements of our Momentum Model.

So where does your organization's culture stand right now? And what steps can you take to change or improve it?

Schein believed that "organizational cultures are created by leaders, and one of the most decisive functions of leadership may well be the creation, the management, and—if and when that may become necessary—the destruction of culture." He recognized that this isn't easy, though. "Changing the culture of a group is very difficult, not because people consciously resist new ways, but because of the unexamined assumptions they hold and the comfort that comes from the shared meaning those assumptions provide."

To maintain and strengthen a culture, Schein stresses that it has to be reinforced through "every human interaction within the organization." He outlines several steps leaders can take to manage and transform culture effectively.

- *Assessment:* Leaders must assess the current culture by identifying artifacts, espoused values, and underlying assumptions.

- *Alignment:* Leaders should align organizational structures, processes, and practices with the desired culture.

- *Communication:* Consistent communication of the desired culture through stories, symbols, and rituals is crucial

- *Role Modeling:* Leaders need to embody the desired culture through their actions and decisions.

- *Reinforcement:* Reward systems and recognition should reinforce behaviors that align with the desired culture.

- *Evolution:* Recognizing that culture change is a gradual process, leaders must be patient and persistent in their efforts.

"Culture eats strategy for breakfast," said management guru Peter Drucker. And that rings true. You can have the best playbook, the most skilled players, but if they don't buy into the culture, it's not going to work.

In 2024, Nvidia ranked number one in Indiggo's "Return on Leadership" scorecard, resulting primarily from the company's high scores in strategic clarity, leadership alignment, and focused action—factors that mirror Schein's research and create the most fertile ground, or potential energy, for momentum.

Leadership influences a team's direction, alignment, and level of commitment. But culture serves as the vehicle for how people elect to behave over time. Leaders must reinforce the behaviors and norms (for example, setting measurable subgoals) that set the conditions for generating positive momentum while also stamping out the behaviors that allow negative momentum to continue unabated (for example, allowing a lack of accountability). Getting the right people placed in your critical roles and holding them accountable for their teams' behaviors over time is how you build a supportive culture (as opposed to one that holds the team back from doing the things required to seize upon momentum or reverse it when trending in the wrong direction).

B efore coaching the Warriors, Steve Kerr was a player himself. By 2003, he had played for six different NBA teams under six different head coaches. So, while he had never coached a team himself, he was no stranger to the various styles and approaches professional coaches take. He'd no doubt gained perspective on what he thought worked, and didn't, and brought to his team a style that translated to phenomenal, sustainable momentum on the court and palpable joy while doing so.

What would a culture of joy look like in your organization?

The Burke-Litwin Change Model examines eleven factors that influence individual and organizational performance. One of the components of their model is organizational culture. Burke and Litwin identified several questions one should explore in service of identifying a "relatively enduring set of values and norms that underlie a social system." The following five questions are a sample of ones the model related to culture:

1. Does your organization have a distinct, apparent, readily identifiable culture? If so, what words would you use to describe it?

2. What seems to drive people in this organization (or what is it that consistently gets people's attention)?

3. To what extent are organizational members clear about "how we do things here"?

4. To what extent are organizational members treated with respect and dignity?

5. Is conflict surfaced and managed, or is it avoided?

LEADER ACTIONS

E dgar Schein once said, "The only thing of real importance that leaders do is to create and manage culture." Sociologists generally highlight that culture consists of the values, beliefs, systems of language, communication, and practices that people share in common and that can be used to define them as a collective. Consequently, how teams will respond to environmental stimuli is a function of how they've been acculturated to behave. It is important to understand that culture is "leader business," and approaching it with intentionality is critical.

Schein's work classified five things (that is, primary mechanisms) as the most powerful drivers one can leverage in service of modifying culture. The five items are as follows: what leaders pay attention to, measure, and control; leader reactions to critical incidents and organizational crises; deliberate role modeling, teaching, and coaching; criteria for allocation of rewards and status; organizational design and structure. Using these behaviors will be key when undertaking the following proposed actions related to fostering momentum.

ACTION 1:
Ensure your teams routinely reflect on their actions.

The process of decision-making, reflection, and refinement is a symbiotic relationship, each influencing the other in a continuous loop. To learn faster and more effectively, teams must properly utilize proven reflection techniques regularly. For example, the US military conducts "In-Progress Reviews and After-Action Reviews" (IPR/AAR) throughout their activities in order to foster more effective decision-making. The IPR/AAR generally examines four questions: What was supposed to happen? What did happen? What accounts for things that transpired? What can we change the next time? The IPR/AAR is not intended to evaluate success or failure but rather to identify areas for improvement and strengths that can be maintained.

ACTION 2:
Embed agility behaviors into your culture.

The ability to seize momentum (or reverse it) requires challenging the status quo. Some cultures prize stability and others celebrate agility. Creating norms that celebrate agility-related behaviors (for example, collaboration, speed of decision-making, trial tolerance) is crucial if you are to seize upon the opportunities presented in a dynamic environment.

ACTION 3:
Ensure your culture prizes accountability.

The word *accountability* has a negative connotation in many organizations. In the most effective organizations, accountability is *the* word. Seizing momentum requires a staunch adherence toward leaning into designated behaviors. Peter Bregman published a wonderful contribution to management literature in a January 2016 article for *Harvard Business Review* discussing the topic of accountability. The piece delineated five actions required to foster accountability: establish clear expectations, create clear capability, ensure clear measurement, provide clear feedback, and ensure clear consequences. It is important that leaders reinforce these five behaviors.

6
Recruitment

U sually when a team wins a pivotal game in the last second, the postgame locker room is full of unbridled energy. Not so on May 13, 1994. Immediately after the Chicago Bulls pulled out a dramatic victory over the New York Knicks in game 3 of the Eastern Conference semifinals at Chicago Stadium, the winning locker room was grim and heavy. Though the last few seconds of the game had secured a Bulls win, they had also revealed friction within the team from which that year's squad would never recover.

With the series tied 1–1, the game tied at 102–102 with 1.8 seconds remaining in regulation, "Zen Master" coach Phil Jackson called a time-out to draw up the final play. Everyone expected that the play would be designed for Scottie Pippen, one of the best all-around players in NBA history, to take the final shot and finish as the hero. But Jackson—known nearly as much for his Buddhist philosophy as for his strategic approach to the game—decided otherwise. He chose to design the play for Toni Kukoc, a talented Croatian player who had joined the Bulls that season and had a knack for making clutch shots. Pippen would be used as a decoy in the play's design.

Feeling slighted and disrespected by Jackson's decision, Pippen refused to reenter the game. He declined to get off the bench and be part of the play. This was a shocking move, especially considering the high stakes. Even though Pippen wasn't to be the focus of the play, his absence from the court could surely have compromised the success of

Jackson's strategy in various ways—the least of which was in the possibility that Pippen on the sidelines could serve as a clue to the opposition.

But with Pippen on the bench, the play went on as planned. Toni Kukoc received the inbound pass from Pete Myers and hit a remarkable, game-winning jump shot, giving the Bulls a 104–102 victory. But the clamor of the win was overshadowed by Pippen's act of selfish defiance. Everyone felt it—the players, the fans, the media. Pippen's teammates were livid, none more than Bill Cartwright, one of the team's veteran leaders. Cartwright wasn't one to express emotion loudly or often, but the spontaneous speech he gave in the Bulls locker room that day would stick in the minds of those who heard it for decades to come.

With tears streaming down his face, Cartwright called his team together. He couldn't let Pippen's decision to abandon his teammates at a critical moment go without response—surely, it couldn't become the norm or be seen as a model to follow for others. He expressed profound disappointment in Pippen's move, which ran contrary to his concept of team culture—one where players could rely on one another and where wins are shared, regardless of which role any individual player had. He was equally angry at Pippen's display of disrespect toward Jackson as he was toward his fellow teammates, and he urged Pippen to apologize to the team and coach alike. Jackson also addressed what had happened, acknowledging Pippen's value to the team but underscoring the need for every player to trust and follow the coach's decisions. Pippen ultimately did apologize, though many sensed it wasn't genuine, and the incident left a lasting mark on his legacy.

Despite then having the series lead 2–1, the Bulls ultimately lost to the Knicks in the playoffs.

It had been the first season after Michael Jordan's first retirement from the Bulls, leaving the team without its iconic leader. Scottie

Pippen openly expressed how he intended to fill that role. As Jordan's sidekick, Pippen was remarkable for his versatility, defensive prowess, and ability to facilitate the offense. He was a seven-time NBA All-Star, a member of the NBA's 50th Anniversary All-Time Team, and a key figure in the Bulls' six championships during the 1990s. But when he was counted on as the "leader," Pippen's individual greatness found itself clashing with team dynamics. His self-oriented style and desire for recognition caused friction within the team.

Many within basketball never saw Pippen the same way after that moment.

Is it possible to be both a great star and a great teammate? For coaches who are searching for that combination—the player who is individually exceptional but equally capable of celebrating the wins of others—finding those unicorns is important when building that thing we call "team momentum."

This is why filling a roster, a company, a campaign, or a battalion with the right talent is paramount.

A s authors, we acknowledge that this part of the model is what twists most leaders into a pretzel. They want talent. They need talent. But when it comes to recruiting or putting together a team that can seize a moment and turn it into momentum, that talent has to be willing to prioritize team goals over personal stats.

For momentum to really take off, teammates need to genuinely celebrate when someone else on the team does something big for the greater good. If even one person on your team sees someone else getting praise and reacts negatively—whether they internalize it or, even worse, act out because the big moment wasn't theirs—it can completely douse the spark. Some might call this "pulling a Pippen." That one small reaction can stop momentum in its tracks.

People are always the key. A 2012 McKinsey global survey, part of the "War for Talent" study, measured the productivity gap between average and high performers based on how complex their job was. In low-complexity jobs, high performers were 50 percent more productive than average ones. But in highly complex roles, the productivity difference was an astounding 800 percent! In short, finding top talent really matters.

But it's not just about having great people on your team—it's about having the right people in the right roles. That's where things really come together. A 2005 *Harvard Business Review* article, "'A Players' or 'A Positions'?: The Strategic Logic of Workforce Management," by Mark Huselid, Dick Beatty, and Brian Becker, created a framework for pinpointing the roles that are absolutely essential to driving your organization's strategy. They referred to these as "A positions."

While it might be tempting to fill your whole team with A players, it's rare for an organization to be built that way. Instead, Huselid and his coauthors advise that leaders focus on strategically placing top talent in these critical A roles, which are the ones that will have the biggest impact on your success. Consequently, they said the following regarding what leaders should strive to enact regarding talent:

> While conventional wisdom might argue that the firms with the most talent win, we believe that, given the financial and managerial resources needed to attract, select, develop, and retain high performers, companies simply can't afford to have A players in all positions. Rather, we believe that the firms with the right talent win. Businesses need to adopt a portfolio approach to workforce management, placing the very best employees in strategic positions, good performers in support

positions, and eliminating nonperforming employees and jobs that don't add value.

The graphic below highlights the distinction between A roles that require A talent.

	A Position STRATEGIC	B Position SUPPORT	C Position SURPLUS
DEFINING CHARACTERISTICS	Has a direct strategic impact AND Exhibits high performance variability among those in the position, representing upside potential	Has an indirect strategic impact by supporting strategic positions and minimizes downside risk by providing a foundation for strategic efforts OR Has a potential strategic impact but exhibits little performance variability among those in the position	May be required for the firm to function but has little strategic impact
Scope of authority	Autonomous decision-making	Specific processes or procedures typically must be followed	Little discretion in work
Primary determinant of compensation	Performance	Job level	Market price
Effect on value creation	Creates value by substantially enhancing revenue or reducing costs	Supports value-creating positions	Has little positive economic impact
Consequences of mistakes	May be very costly, but missed revenue opportunities are a greater loss to the firm	May be very costly and can destroy value	Not necessarily costly

	A Position STRATEGIC	B Position SUPPORT	C Position SURPLUS
Consequences of hiring the wrong person	Significant expense in terms of lost investment and revenue opportunities	Fairly easily remedied through hiring of replacement	Easily remedied through hiring of replacement

I f you knew the name David Ross before the 2012 Major League Baseball season, it would prove you were one of the sport's great fans. Though Ross would go on to a fifteen-year MLB career, he spent all but two seasons of that time as a backup catcher bouncing among several teams. But Ross would become the exemplar of this module on recruiting.

Halfway through his career, he earned that starting role with the Cincinnati Reds. When the Reds changed managers, bringing in Dusty Baker as leader, Baker noticed something about Ross that didn't sit well with him. He felt his catcher had become more concerned about his personal statistics than he was team success. To make the point, he yanked Ross from the field in the middle of the game and replaced him with his backup. The move led to an animated conversation after the game where Ross demanded an explanation.

The result: Baker cut Ross from the team weeks before the season's end.

Ross was given a short stint in Boston with the Red Sox, but when the team's playoff run ended short of the World Series, General Manager Theo Epstein privately let Ross know he wouldn't be invited back the following year. Then he offered a moment most leaders don't give departing employees. "You should know," Epstein began, "that when we looked at bringing you here, we called Cincinnati. The word we got was that we shouldn't add you to the team because you're a bad teammate. That's not what we saw in the last few weeks, but that's your reputation. And in this business, reputations die hard."

Ross left the meeting stunned. But rather than blame his former manager, he set out to change his reputation. When he landed with the Braves in Atlanta, he started asking every player in the locker room to tell them about the best teammate they ever played with and to give him three words to describe that teammate. He made a list of characteristics—encouraging, mentoring, truthful, and fully present among others—and set out to bring those to the field every day.

Over the next four years when he played as a backup in Atlanta, he fully transformed the way others saw him. He was always standing on the top step of the dugout, praising teammates for great play. That made him a player that younger talent sought out for advice. And as his contract in Atlanta expired, fully half of the teams in baseball lined up to sign him to a deal. He was a backup . . . but he was the glue that could hold a team together.

He went back to Boston, where he helped the Red Sox win the 2013 Series. Then he went to Chicago, where he helped the Cubs do the same in 2016. As the seventh game of that 2016 Series came to a close, the player who was lifted by teammates to their shoulders and carried from the field: David Ross, a backup catcher.

"I learned so much on that journey," Ross said for this book. "Every team needs talent. But what they also need are players who will make others better just by the words they say and the way they carry themselves. You have to bring those players to your team to find real success."

Ross would go on to manage the Cubs for three years, and he said he was always looking to recruit players who would offer selflessness as a skill.

S ue Semrau got silent. It was the first time in over an hour where our conversation about momentum simply stopped. The shared energy and animation about preparation, communication, culture, and leadership for momentum had been palpable. One idea flowed to the next; examples and thoughts intermingled. Stories. Theories. Visualizations of what momentum looked and felt like. But then we asked about recruitment, and the ability for coaches to seek talent that not only can perform well on the court but also has the right fit in terms of personality.

Coach Semrau—who had transformed the Florida State Seminoles into a formidable force in women's college basketball, leading the team to numerous NCAA tournament appearances and earning multiple ACC Coach of the Year honors—seemed to play out various responses in her head, perhaps some contradictory to others, before choosing to respond with a question: "In an ideal world with no constraints? Sure. We would love to recruit for personality."

She paused, her eyes reflecting a mix of resolve and contemplation. "But it's never that simple."

Recruiting players for college basketball teams involves navigating numerous challenges and constraints. Some key difficulties and limitations faced by programs and coaches, we learned, include high demand and recruiting wars where the best high school players are flooded with promises of playing time, development opportunities, and exposure. Then there's the academic requirements set by the NCAA that can disqualify otherwise talented players and admissions standards held by some schools, which can further limit the pool of potential recruits. The NCAA itself sets stringent rules governing recruitment, including limits on contact periods, official visits, and permissible benefits, and programs must be vigilant in monitoring compliance to avoid violations that could lead to sanctions. Programs are further restricted by the number of scholarships they can offer, and there are financial limits on how much programs can spend on recruiting activities. Then there's the increasing use of the transfer portal, which allows players to move more freely between programs, adding another layer of complexity to recruiting and retention. Parents and other influencers often have significant input into a recruit's decision, which can complicate the recruitment process. Coaches must navigate external pressures and sometimes unrealistic expectations from family and advisers.

There's only so many spots, and sometimes the players who fit the positions that need recruiting don't have the right personalities or meet the academic criteria. The coach's hands are often tied. In other words, it's hard enough to find talent to match an open position. The rest is icing—or must be created, and fostered, once the recruit is signed. That's where Coach Semrau thrived—in raising her new players into the team culture and, for lack of a better phrase, making it work.

Semrau's career was a testament to her philosophy. When she took over the FSU women's basketball program in 1997, it was struggling. But she saw potential where others saw problems. Her approach to recruitment was holistic. She didn't just look for talented players; she looked for individuals who would contribute positively to the team's culture.

Under her leadership, the Seminoles became known not just for their skill on the court but for their unity and resilience off it. She instituted regular team-building exercises, encouraged open communication, and fostered a sense of family among her players. This culture of trust and mutual respect was integral to their success.

Coach Semrau shared stories of recruits who had initially seemed like perfect fits based on their stats and performance but who had struggled to adapt to the team culture. Conversely, there were those who might not have been the most highly sought-after recruits but who flourished in the supportive, disciplined environment Semrau cultivated. Semrau's success wasn't just measured in wins and losses but in the lasting impact she had on her players. Many of her former athletes went on to have successful careers, both in basketball and beyond, carrying with them the lessons learned under her guidance.

As Semrau reflected on her recruitment strategies and the enormous number of variables that make this process particularly challenging, it was clear that her silence at the beginning of our discussion wasn't a hesitation born of disdain but more a reflection of the deep respect she holds for the role of recruitment, and the constraints that make it even more important to get right.

When thinking about recruitment, it is easy to focus on a leader's initial assembly of a team—bringing people in to form a team from the ground up, perhaps even all at a common time. In practice, however, recruitment is an ongoing exercise. Not all leaders have the chance to create a team from scratch. Rather, most inherit players, soldiers, candidates, or staff who are already on board. Many leaders have extreme limitations on how they can attract new blood and have little control over the characteristics of those in the pools from which they select. Therefore, the challenge is to create an optimal balance of personalities and skills within a team through mindful, strategic recruitment and preparation. Recruitment also applies within long-tenured teams or organizations where no "new" members are brought in but where a leader identifies or selects individuals for specific tasks within a larger game plan.

Colleges and the military face the immense task of recruiting thousands of individuals at a time. Colleges, for instance, must fill their freshman classes each year, attracting students from diverse backgrounds and academic achievements. The more applicants they recruit, the pickier they can be about who is selected. The military, similarly, recruits a large number of personnel annually to maintain and bolster its ranks. Once recruits meet the basic criteria for enlistment, rigorous physical, academic, and personality testing helps the military determine who does what and where. But at phase one, for these giant organizations, recruitment is a numbers game, and significant quantities can make the cut.

Companies often recruit for a dozen or more positions at a time, focusing on specific roles within their organization. This targeted recruitment requires a somewhat more refined approach compared to mass recruitment, but there are various channels through which to do so: headhunters, job boards, career websites, networking events, and their own platforms—not to mention a roster of existing employees who may grow into roles they didn't start in to begin with.

Then there are smaller businesses or sports teams where there's only one or a few spots open per position. These teams need to be extremely selective, as each recruit can significantly affect the organization's performance. These recruitment efforts benefit from advanced data analytics to assess candidate performance and potential, but with a limited and highly specified talent pool, competition between organizations can be fierce. And finally, in politics—where just one candidate from a party can appear on a final ballot—there's just one seat. This recruitment process is highly strategic and personalized. Sometimes potential candidates wait years if not decades for their turn in line to run for a desired seat.

Whether thousands of recruits or just one, recruitment is pivotal in our model of momentum. To understand how and why, we look first to the science of recruitment.

There is a large body of research that examines the value created by the most productive talent. A 2012 study by Aguinis and Boyle published in *Personal Psychology* examined more than six hundred thousand people operating across a variety of fields like entertainment, research, politics, and athletics. Their study concluded that high performers are 400 percent more productive than average ones. Additionally, researchers have also studied the value generated by getting the right talent in the roles that produce the greatest amount of organizational value.

A great example of the value associated with getting "A-level" talent in the most critical roles was detailed by Sandy Ogg (former chief human resources officer at Unilever and former operating partner at the Blackstone Group) in a 2018 *McKinsey Quarterly* article.

Ogg noted that, during his time at Blackstone, a clear trend emerged among the most successful portfolio companies. Ogg highlighted that 80 percent of the companies who focused immediately on matching the "right talent" to their critical roles from the start achieved all of their first-year targets. Furthermore, those companies averaged a 2.5 multiple return on the initial investment. Ogg's next finding was even more actionable: Of the 180 successful portfolio companies studied, the top twenty-two all made talent decisions by linking key leadership roles to the value they needed to generate. The takeaway? Getting the right people in place, and doing it quickly, plays a huge role in building momentum.

Indeed, there are several academic models and theories that outline the principles of successful recruitment. These models, each based on a different set of underlying assumptions, provide a structured approach to understanding and implementing effective recruitment strategies.

The Person-Organization Fit (P-O Fit) model, advanced by various industrial and organizational psychologists, gained prominence in the 1980s. The model emphasizes the alignment between an individual's values, beliefs, and personality with the organizational culture and values. The better the fit, the more likely the individual will be satisfied, committed, and productive.

The P-O Fit model was used as the basis for a more evolved concept—the Attraction-Selection-Attrition (ASA) framework, proposed by Benjamin Schneider in 1987. This model suggests that organizations attract individuals who share similar values and personalities (attraction), select those who fit the organizational culture (selection), and see those who do not fit often leave the organization (attrition).

Both of these models underscore the assumption that team members who are happy and fulfilled in their work will perform well for the organization and that recruitment should begin with recruiting for fulfillment. Offshoots of these models suggest that people seek to join organizations where they perceive a sense of belonging and identity. Organizations, therefore, should recruit individuals who identify with their brand, mission, and social groups within the organization and should create and advertise jobs that are meaningful, provide autonomy, and offer opportunities for skill variety, task identity, and feedback.

Other models of recruitment look more at the functional needs of an organization. The Resource-Based View posits that organizations should recruit individuals who provide unique skills and competencies that are valuable, rare, inimitable, and nonsubstitutable. These resources contribute to a sustainable competitive advantage. Similarly, the Human Capital Theory and the Competency-Based Recruitment Model both focus on recruiting individuals with the knowledge, skills, and abilities, or specific competencies, required for the job—which include not only technical skills but also behavioral attributes like communication, teamwork, and leadership.

Jim Collins's concept of "getting the right people on the bus" in his book *Good to Great* aligns closely with several aspects of the P-O Fit model and the ASA framework. Collins emphasizes the importance of having the right people who share the core values and vision of the organization. This aligns with the P-O Fit model, which stresses the alignment between an individual's values, beliefs, and personality with the organizational culture and values. Collins notes that great companies focus on "first who, then what," meaning they first get the right people on the bus (in the organization) and the wrong people off, and then figure out where to drive it (strategic direction).

Collins's idea that the right people are those who are not only capable but also passionately committed to the organization's mission parallels the ASA framework. According to the ASA model, organizations attract, select, and retain individuals who are a good fit with their culture, while those who do not fit well tend to leave. Collins emphasizes hiring based on character and innate capabilities rather than specific knowledge or skills, which resonates with the P-O Fit model's focus on value and cultural alignment. The emphasis on cultural fit over specific job-related skills aligns with both the P-O Fit and ASA models, where fitting into the organizational culture is crucial for long-term success and commitment. And Collins's idea of continually assessing whether team members are still the right fit for the bus mirrors the ASA model's concept of attrition, where those who do not fit well naturally leave the organization.

Military Context

You're almost certainly familiar with the US Army's "Be All You Can Be" and the Marines' "The Few. The Proud." These slogans are part of the US military's multifaceted recruitment theory that integrates elements from various recruitment and human resource management models, with a particular emphasis on strategic, psychological, and practical considerations.

The military seeks to attract individuals who are drawn to the values and lifestyle of military service and those who meet stringent physical and mental criteria. Where in a business or sports environment, attrition may happen gradually or over time, the military front-loads attrition as much as possible. Basic training serves as both an introduction to military life and a further selection process where those not suited for military service are identified. In other words, the military seeks to quickly identify those who do not fit well and give them an early out.

The employment of assessment center practices enhances the military's ability to solidify their recruit retention success rate. For example, the Armed Services Vocational Aptitude Battery Test assesses candidates' faculties in verbal, math, science, technology, and spatial areas. Medical examinations, physical fitness tests, and security background checks are other examples of frontloaded practices the military employs in comprehensive manner to get the "right" people into its ranks. Beyond measurable skills, the military also seeks to recruit a diverse workforce to reflect the society it serves and to benefit from a wide range of perspectives and skill—something that lends significantly to its culture.

From there, the military invests in recruits as valuable assets. The military provides extensive training and education to enhance the skills and capabilities of its personnel, ensuring they can meet the demands of their roles. There's enormous focus on retaining skilled personnel by offering career development opportunities, competitive benefits, and support for personal and professional growth.

Political Context

Political recruitment is a complex and strategic process that has been the topic of significant academic research across various fields. In theory, integrating insights from behavioral sciences, leadership theories, diversity research, data analytics, and political science, political parties and organizations can develop more effective recruitment strategies to identify, attract, and support candidates who are likely to succeed in the political arena.

And there are some efforts to do so. Increasingly, political machines are using big data analysis to understand the traits and qualities that appeal to voters, to understand the psychological traits that make for effective leaders, and to identify potential candidates based on demographics, social media activity, and public engagement.

But in practice, political recruitment is messier. Parties often establish search committees to identify potential candidates. Polls and focus groups are used to gauge public opinion and identify desirable candidate traits. Potential candidates are persuaded to run through a combination of appeals to their sense of duty, party loyalty, and personal ambition. Extensive vetting (ideally) ensures they can withstand public scrutiny, but vetting is almost always incomplete or imperfect and gives an entity a view of only what's already happened in a candidate's life—not what's to come.

And here's the real kicker: In politics, an individual can effectively nominate themselves for public consideration. Even if a party organization goes through a rigorous process to select one candidate to run for a seat as its nominee, other members of that same party can file to run too. Party organizations are often under constraints to appear neutral (at least as far as the public can tell) in primary elections, which can restrict the effectiveness of party elites in advancing the one person they *really* want in office.

If they can get that person to agree to run at all.

Perhaps the most notable reluctant candidate of all time was Dwight D. Eisenhower, who became the thirty-fourth president of the United States. Eisenhower had a distinguished career as a military officer. He graduated from West Point in 1915 and rose through the ranks of the US Army. During World War II, Eisenhower served as the supreme commander of the Allied Expeditionary Forces in Europe, where he led the successful invasion of Normandy (D-Day) and played a crucial role in the defeat of Nazi Germany. Despite his military success, Eisenhower had no political experience and initially showed little interest in a political career. His leadership during World War II made him a national hero, respected by both the public and political leaders across the spectrum—all of which made him an attractive candidate for public office.

The idea of Eisenhower running for president began to take shape in the late 1940s. Both parties wanted him—something we'd rarely find today—and both the Democratic and Republican parties sought to recruit Eisenhower as a presidential candidate. President Harry S. Truman even considered asking Eisenhower to run as a Democrat in 1948.

But Eisenhower was extremely reluctant to enter politics. In fact, he continually refused. He had never been involved in partisan politics and was more focused on his military and administrative duties, including his role as president of Columbia University. Eisenhower valued his nonpartisan status and feared that entering politics might tarnish his reputation as a unifying national figure.

Despite his reluctance, or perhaps even in part because of it, a grass-roots movement known as "Draft Eisenhower" began to gain momentum. Citizens from various walks of life, including veterans, business leaders, and everyday Americans, saw Eisenhower as the ideal candidate to lead the nation through the complexities of the postwar era. They believed that his leadership skills, integrity, and nonpartisan stance made him uniquely qualified to unite the country. Several influential figures played crucial roles in the Draft Eisenhower movement. Among them were prominent politicians like Senator Henry Cabot Lodge Jr., who saw Eisenhower as the Republican Party's best hope against the Democrats in the 1952 election. Lodge, along with others, organized committees and rallies to garner support for Eisenhower's candidacy.

Intense grassroots mobilization began. Supporters created "Eisenhower for President" clubs across the country, collecting signatures and organizing rallies to demonstrate widespread public support. Newspapers, radio shows, and magazines were utilized to promote Eisenhower as a candidate, despite his lack of interest, highlighting his leadership during World War II and his potential to bring stability and prosperity to the nation. Influential politicians and public figures publicly endorsed Eisenhower, adding credibility and momentum to the draft movement.

Eisenhower began to see the presidency as a continuation of his service to the country. He was convinced that his leadership was needed to navigate the Cold War, combat communism, and manage domestic challenges. The widespread call to duty resonated with his sense of patriotism. Republican leadership assured Eisenhower that he would have significant autonomy in his administration and the support needed to implement his vision for the country.

In January 1952, after much contemplation and encouragement from his closest advisers and family, Eisenhower finally agreed to run for president. He announced his candidacy and entered the Republican primaries, eventually securing the nomination.

The Draft Eisenhower effort is an extraordinary example of momentum in practice—a rare case where momentum *preceded* a political win by convincing the right candidate to enter the fray, as opposed to the usual course of events where a person opts themselves in and desires momentum to push their campaign along.

When Bob McDonald took over as secretary of the Department of Veterans Affairs in 2014, he inherited an agency mired in scandal and dysfunction. The VA had been plagued by reports of widespread mismanagement and systemic failures, most notably in the form of extensive delays in veterans receiving medical care. Some had been waiting months, even years, to receive care. This situation came to a head in April 2014 when whistleblowers exposed that veterans at the Phoenix VA hospital had died while waiting for care and that VA employees had manipulated records to hide the long wait times. Rather than an isolated issue involving one or a few bad actors, the practice of falsifying records to make wait times appear shorter than they were was widespread. This dishonesty was enabled by a culture lacking accountability or consequence.

These revelations led to a massive public and political outcry. Veterans groups, lawmakers, and the general public demanded immediate reforms, and the VA came under intense scrutiny from Congress, with numerous hearings held to investigate the issues and determine responsibility. The media kept a spotlight on the VA's failures, ensuring that the pressure for reform remained high. And this spotlight was never brighter than when McDonald took the reins.

Bob McDonald didn't just slingshot himself into top leadership roles—not in his thirty-three years at Procter & Gamble and not in the US Army. Rather, McDonald was an example of rising through the ranks, learning each role with deep involvement before being tapped to take on the next challenge. McDonald began his career as a student at the US Military Academy at West Point, graduating in 1975 with a degree in engineering.

McDonald worked hard enough as a cadet at West Point to become highly decorated and graduate in the top 2 percent of his class, yet he started back at the bottom in his first assignment as an Army Airborne Ranger. He went to the 82nd Airborne Division as a second lieutenant. Eventually, he became the assistant operations officer of a battalion where he helped lead warfare training near the Arctic Circle. He managed to earn an MBA while leading his troops, and upon leaving the military, he once again returned to the lowest ranks as he began a career in business.

He joined Procter & Gamble in 1980 as a brand assistant for Tide, an entry-level position that gave him experience in marketing and ad campaigns, before being promoted to brand manager, where he conducted research and managed performance in the market. Later, McDonald was sent to the Philippines and then to Japan. He served as vice president and general manager in those markets, taking on significant leadership in challenges in each location. He returned to the United States as president of Global Fabric Care before being pinned as the organization's chief operating officer, then president and CEO, and then chairman of the board. Under his leadership, P&G added nearly one billion people to its global customer base, and its stock price increased by 60 percent in his four years as CEO.

In other words, McDonald hadn't just led but had worked in every level of the organization—a feature that appealed strongly to

President Barack Obama when he appointed McDonald to one of the biggest agency messes of his administration. Indeed, when McDonald arrived at the VA, it was clearly critically understaffed, particularly in the areas of medical care and administrative support. McDonald also observed a severe leadership vacuum at many VA facilities, rendering them ineffective or in disarray. And at the topmost levels, there was a lack of empowered leadership to address systemic issues and implement necessary reforms. McDonald's first step was to embark on a "listening tour," visiting VA facilities across the country to hear directly from veterans and VA employees about the problems they faced. Concurrently, McDonald emphasized accountability and transparency, pledging to fire any employee found to have engaged in misconduct or to have failed in their duties.

He is solidly crafted in the mold of the servant leader, one who leads from the front. And one of the many ways McDonald builds the trust needed for this kind of leadership is to give out his personal phone number.

"When I became the leader at the VA, I needed to create trust. In a crisis, a leader has to be even more accessible," said McDonald. "One weekend, a veteran called me, and I referred him to our Suicide Prevention Hotline. As I recall, they intervened, and the veteran's alive today. I haven't changed the phone number. And I still answer it today."

But at the core of what was necessary for McDonald to accomplish was a shift in recruitment: hiring more medical professionals and administrative staff, and hiring leaders who could effectively and transparently manage the organization with a strenuous commitment to accountability.

This was an overwhelming undertaking. It is estimated that McDonald proposed the removal of more than nine hundred employees during his first two years in office. This included the replacement of senior leaders within the VA and appointing new directors at some of the most troubled VA facilities. Recruiting for these roles—both in mass and for specific, niche roles—was not easy. Many new, talented people were brought in, but one new hire, in particular, stood out to McDonald: David Shulkin, recruited to serve as undersecretary for health, a critical role overseeing the Veterans Health Administration. Shulkin was a physician with extensive experience in health care management—described as one of the "high priests" of patient-centered care and the type of executive who would walk the floors of his hospitals on night shifts to ensure proper care was being given.

McDonald recognized in Shulkin qualities that made him an ideal candidate for helping transform the culture of the organization. For starters, Shulkin had a collaborative style and an exceptional ability to work effectively with different types of people, including health care professionals, policymakers, and veterans themselves. McDonald saw Shulkin's humility and compassion—an empathy that extended to veterans and their families. He would go the extra mile to understand individual concerns and needs, and he valued transparency in both his personal conduct and in the process through which he'd make decisions. Despite his high rank, Shulkin was approachable and grounded. He was hands-on and, like McDonald, a team player.

Recruiting one's successor may be one of the great acts of professional humility, and in McDonald's selection of Shulkin, this, too, was true. Shulkin went on to become secretary of the VA, continuing McDonald's legacy.

"Life is a series of starting over," McDonald told us. "Life is a series of chapters, and you as an individual have to have confidence in yourself that you aren't afraid to start over."

Amy Howe, CEO of FanDuel, perhaps said it best in our interview on leadership and momentum. "The most important thing for me was to make sure that I could build the best leadership team around me," Howe shared, describing how she'd recruited from within the ranks of her company—many who had been there since before sports betting was even legal—while looking to identify where they needed to bring in some new talent to the organization. "It doesn't matter how good I am; I don't scale as an individual."

The Pareto principle (also known as the 80/20 rule) is a phenomenon that states that roughly 80 percent of outcomes come from 20 percent of causes. Frequently, the principle is discussed in the vein of understanding one's most important customers and the revenue they provide. Yet there is a body of research that suggests the 80/20 rule also has implications for organizational talent. Finding the "right" people who possess the required capabilities and buy in to your principles is essential. Such people will drive the organizational actions required to foster and seize momentum.

ACTION 1:
Identify your most critical roles and ensure you get the right people in those seats.

A 2017 McKinsey Insight article encouraged leaders to "focus on the 5 percent who deliver 95 percent of the value." Certain roles play a far larger part in generating organizational success than many others. Here is an example of this concept from the McKinsey article: "Let's consider American football. If you asked people who is the most highly paid player on a team, they would correctly say the quarterback, the key person in the vast majority of plays. People would probably say that the second most highly paid player was the running back or the wide receiver, since they work directly with the quarterback to advance the ball. These people are wrong. It's the relatively unnoticed left tackle, who protects a right-handed quarterback's blind side from things he can't see and could injure him."

ACTION 2:
Ensure your onboarding process is comprehensive and geared around the actual work to be performed.

Great onboarding helps your new team members learn about the company's culture and prepare for their employment. It also includes a plan of performance expectations for their first few months, which helps them focus and create momentum in their discrete roles.

ACTION 3:
Routinely evaluate the effectiveness of your recruitment process.

Continually seeking to refine your team's ability to find the right talent is of the utmost importance. Merely mimicking the actions of how other organizations recruit talent will not ensure great outcomes for your team. Routine and rigorous examination of your process will help immensely to enhance it.

7

Preparation

When we rang Buzz Williams at 9:00 a.m. on a Wednesday morning, it was already midday for the famed basketball coach. He had already completed the Wednesday version of his daily workout routine—the days where he begins outdoors. It was a habit he started following his second year of coaching at Marquette right after he landed himself a three-day stay at the Mayo Clinic at the end of the season. Batteries of tests showed nothing specifically wrong with Williams—just the compounded effects of not sleeping right, not eating right, not handling stress.

He started figuring out what would work, and by the time he was named head coach at Virginia Tech, the wellness regimen was well established.

"I'll be in here every morning at 5:00 a.m.," Williams told his players and staff about the gym, and then he told us about how he made good on that promise. "I haven't missed a day. However many years, no matter what, no matter what, I don't miss a day. When we go on the road, we spend the night in a hotel. The next morning, we go to a local privately owned gym. And we train. That's our 'get better' group. We take a picture of it and post it on social media. So we've created some traditions relative to our health, relative to our fitness. And I think that the players know it's serious to me, because I do the same thing they do. I have the same cycle in the weight room that they do. So I have a pretty good feel for what their body's going through."

From this level of self-discipline it should be no surprise, then, that Buzz Williams approaches the training and preparation of his team in a way few other coaches have endeavored. Also rare is that Williams explicitly weaves the concept of momentum into his team's training, a feature that reflects not only the belief that momentum is real, and tangible, but that it can be prepared for—or even that preparation can make it happen.

Williams coined his model "Time, Score, Momentum" (TSM) and walked us through how this works.

"Time" refers primarily to the management of the game clock. This involves strategic use of time-outs and substitutions to maximize efficiency and effectiveness during the game, and it requires a deep understanding of when to speed up or slow down the game based on the situation, opponent, and flow.

"Score" means constant awareness of the score and using this data to influence decision-making. This includes knowing when to play aggressively or conservatively and identifying and capital- izing on high-percentage scoring opportunities while minimizing low-percentage shots.

Finally, "Momentum" requires the ability of players to recognize shifts in energy during the game and to make strategic moves to either sustain positive momentum or halt negative swings. This requires the maintenance of high levels of focus throughout the game, with play- ers staying mentally engaged and resilient, especially during critical moments.

It's the latter piece that may take the most effort to learn. Whereas time and score are quantitative elements that can be fairly easily mea- sured or observed, momentum is a qualitative experience. The percep- tion of momentum can vary between players, if some can feel it at all.

Getting a team on the same page regarding what momentum looks and feels like is a challenge Williams was determined to tackle. And here's how he did it.

Beyond regimented practice sessions that include fundamental drills, the use of game situation scenarios, and extensive conditioning, Williams incorporates the use of video analysis in novel ways. In this, players watch videos of their own performances to identify strengths and areas for improvement—during which Williams encourages self-critique and reflection. And it includes opponent analysis, including rigorous examination of how opponents operate and perform. In these sessions, Williams will pause plays and rewind, calling on players to share what they're observing and to identify the conditions that preceded momentum.

"I'll stop the clip more often than I will actually play it, because I want to see how each person is processing the information in real time, particularly when they're seeing it for the first time," Williams shared. One player's observation of a meaningful moment can shape how others see the same phenomenon, and through extensive watching, pausing, discussion, and repetition, a sense of shared perception between team members develops. And this video work isn't limited to basketball, either. Williams shows his players clips from other sports. Why? Because their minds are more open.

"Using TSM in other sports may even be more meaningful to our guys," Williams explained. "You know, if I show our kids a clip of an NBA team, well, they know that they follow that guy on social media, right? Oh, they're wearing his shoes. They don't like him. He's a crybaby. And so they're narrow in a lot of their opinions. And yeah, opinions come into play. But if I show him Oregon State or Arkansas baseball, it's easier to ask—what do you see? What was the fingertip, the spark that changed everything?"

Williams again and again and again has his players watch clips of themselves and others simply to find that spark. "We have to create an environment that recognizes the spark," he said. "If you can't sense the spark, there is no spark. So I train them to watch and say, 'Let's get out there and feel our way around. And let's see if we can find the spark.'"

"In my own illogical way, this is what I think momentum is," mused basketball coach Kevin Eastman, "the surge that occurs when practice and preparation meets near perfection."

Similar to Buzz Williams, Eastman's focus on practice is distinguished by meticulous planning, emphasis on mental conditioning, and data. He creates simulations of specific situations players might encounter during a game, such as end-of-quarter plays, defensive stances, and fast-break opportunities. But more than anything, Eastman is rare in his focus on the minutiae of the game, such as footwork, positioning, and timing. He meticulously studies opponents, breaking down their strategies, strengths, and weaknesses to create detailed game plans.

The best organizations understand the importance of preparing for pivotal moments. One surprising insight that emerged from our interviews and conversations is how many people think success comes from simply waiting for an opportunity to arise. But if you wait without preparation, you won't be in the best position to capitalize when it happens. In sports and the military, much of the work revolves around being ready for various scenarios, yet this concept has caught some in the business world off guard.

The key to success lies not just in having a plan for the opportunity but in cultivating the right mindset to seize it. Coaches like

Buzz Williams emphasize this by running practice drills that simulate high-pressure situations, such as being down with only a few seconds left on the clock. It's about both game planning and instilling the belief in players that, even in the toughest circumstances, good outcomes are possible. This mindset allows individuals to be mentally prepared to perform at their best when the moment arrives.

The military concept of "seizing the initiative" (setting and dictating the terms of action) is articulated in *Army Doctrine Publication 3-0, Unified Land Operations*. It is based on the notion that Army units "seize, retain, and exploit the initiative," while accepting smart risk in service of gaining a position of relative advantage over an adversary. Army units routinely conduct rigorous preparatory exercises designed to hone their ability to seize the initiative when a situation is ripe for doing so. The exercises cover a range of scenarios spanning from the most likely course of action to the most dangerous. Rehearsals are also conducted in order to walk through major decision points while reinforcing what it will take to ensure organizational alignment. In the military, just like in business, sports, and politics, the preferred mode of operation is to be on offense where you are dictating the tempo. Ideally, you want competitors responding to you versus the other way around. Building an organization's ability to accomplish actions effectively is related to the organizational psychology construct of task cohesion (that is, the degree to which members of a group work effectively together to achieve common goals). Rigorous preparation enhances task cohesion (which will heighten the likelihood of being able to impose one's will on an opponent or situation).

Similarly, in business, timing can be everything. For example, executives at Lyft anticipated that Uber's toxic corporate culture would eventually implode, especially during its dominant days. They predicted that when Uber began making headlines for negative reasons, it would create an opportunity for Lyft to step in. So they strategically prepared for that moment. When Uber's front-page controversies started piling up, Lyft was ready to launch a campaign reminding people that ridesharing could still be a safe and positive experience. They were prepared to seize the moment when their competitor faltered.

How can you be ready to seize a moment?

"Oppo research" is a bedrock of preparation in political campaigns— involving deep scrutiny of weaknesses and vulnerabilities, both for one's opponent and oneself. Veteran political consultant and pollster John McLaughlin knows a thing or two about that, often finding himself in the position of educating his candidates about the skeletons in their own closets that his team of researchers has dug up. It's not always met with welcome reception, either.

"Most of the time, our internal research finds more than the candidate discloses," McLaughlin shared. "Sometimes it's important, sometimes it's not. But you have to do it. Sometimes, when you're the candidate, it's hard to think of what might be there—even smart candidates miss their own vulnerabilities."

Other times, candidates know what might be dug up on them but don't think it matters. For example, they might believe a contentious divorce file is sealed only to later discover that someone has a copy or stole one. But for the political consultant, these findings determine whether to take on a client or a race—or stay out—or to advise their candidate on how to best approach the baggage.

"You have to expect the unexpected. So you prepare. And the best way, I find, most often the truth is the best option. If you find a fault, and there's a mea culpa, you gotta do it. If, on the other hand, if you find out something that's fatal, you might go to the candidate and say, 'Save yourself time and money—don't bother running.'"

In McLaughin's thirty-five years in political consulting, he's worked for national and world leaders—Ronald Reagan, Benjamin Netanyahu, Arnold Schwarzenegger, and Donald Trump, to name a few. But, despite the enormity of things he's seen and worked on, to McLaughlin—a math student—the basic goal of a political strategy is simple: The currency is public opinion; generally speaking (although not always), you need to get to 51 percent, and you need momentum to get there.

Preparing for momentum in politics, to McLaughlin, is a bit like calculus. "You have limits—an upper limit and lower limit. And you're operating in those limits. Public opinion, when it gets information, will accelerate and decelerate, just like a curve. I don't think it moves in a straight line; I think it moves like a curve. And there's inflection points. When enough information is out there, and it's not changing public opinion, then you've got to find the next one," he told us. "So when we do surveys for people, we tell them as much as we can find. Certainly everybody wants to know their chances of winning and only after that ask about their strengths and weaknesses. They want to know the key issues that will bring them votes. To consultants, this translates into identifying the critical voter groups that would create a majority coalition, and then you've got to figure out how to use the media to convey information most efficiently."

Through all of these moving parts—these data-driven preparations—political momentum requires continual tracking of progress using whatever measuring sticks are available: donation amounts, number of donors, attendance at rallies, social media engagement, polling, web traffic, and even—yes—yard signs.

"You have to track progress," McLaughlin said. "You always constantly have to be moving toward the majority."

. . .

Across the figurative aisle from John McLaughlin, and across a lit-eral, lively living room from us, James Carville looked out of the picture windows that overlook the Shenandoah Valley. That overlook history itself.

Legend has it that some major traumatic events, like battles in war, can leave behind an energetic imprint on the environment and that this residual energy plays and replays itself out over time, long after the original incident has quieted. To the surprise or discomfort of vis-itors of the Shenandoah Valley, Civil War clashes like at Belle Grove still seem to be getting fought out—by apparitions—giving modern witnesses a supernatural front seat to the sounds of cannons and the shouts of soldiers 160 years later.

No doubt, the horrors of the Civil War left a deep psychological imprint on the nation, perhaps in few places as deeply as in western Virginia—where Union and Confederate territories met and to where pivotal battles reshaped the United States as we know it. The Battle of Belle Grove was part of the wider Shenandoah Valley Campaign of 1864. It began with what looked like a sure Confederate win. These forces, led by Lieutenant General Jubal Early, attacked sleep-ing Union soldiers under heavy fog, before dawn. They captured more than twelve hundred Union prisoners and more than twenty artillery pieces while forcing multiple Union divisions to fall back.

Union major general Philip Sheridan returned from a meeting in Washington, DC, to this scene. He hurried to the battlefield—his arrival both calming and revitalizing his troops. The Union took their time from there; they didn't rush in. Sheridan's team interviewed pris-oners and learned that beneath the surface of the Confederate attack were hungry, exhausted soldiers. They coordinated a plan and reorga-nized. The Union counterattack began just before 4:00 p.m., joined from the right by General G. A. Custer's First Brigade and from the left by Colonel Thomas Devin's Second Brigade.

Confederate troops panicked and fell into disorder. Intense fighting led to a Union victory, forever weakening the Confederacy's position in the Shenandoah Valley—a region they had relied on heavily for supplies. This valley had been considered the "Breadbasket of the Confederacy" due to its rich agricultural assets—wheat, apples, and poultry. Its location was central and provided exceptional cover. But following Belle Grove, never again would Confederate forces be able to maneuver down the valley to threaten the Union capital of Washington, DC.

Momentum had shifted. Not by chance but through strategy and preparation. Through preparing for, seeing, and advancing a spark.

While the region's folklore holds that ghosts occasionally reenact the gruesome fights of the valley's past, on a different type of battleground, that of politics, Carville would know a thing or two about momentum. Few have changed a landscape—of any nature—as dramatically as Carville has done in his field.

Carville invited us into his home for an interview that was about as uncharacteristic as, well, you'd expect given the subject. There wasn't a quiet corner but rather a friendly, constant buzz from the voices of Mary and their friends, and their friends' children. Whether a manifestation of Carville and Matalin's merged energy or in spite of it, the atmosphere was undeniably alive with expectation.

I set the recorder on an end table next to Carville, about as close as it could get. I didn't want to miss a word, but knew I would. We didn't recount his personal story, but I was already familiar with the basics. Long before Carville's distinctive personality, sharp wit, and unapologetic advocacy for his clients made him one of the most recognizable and influential figures in American politics, he had climbed a few hills of his own.

Carville attended Louisiana State University right out of high school but in his own words was "less than an attentive scholar" and "had fifty-six-hours' worth of F's" before he dropped out and joined the United States Marine Corps for a two-year enlistment. Carville then returned to LSU, completing his undergraduate and law degrees, and worked jobs as a high school teacher and attorney before pivoting to his true passion, politics—where the "ranks" and rules are never as clear-cut as they are in the military, and the clients are almost always less manageable than those who ring the bell of a law firm.

But this is exactly the type of field where a rare personality like Carville's thrives.

As with many of the hundreds of interviews we've initiated on this subject, I asked Carville to define momentum. His response was a bit different from the usual. To Carville, momentum in politics is just as much about who has it as who doesn't. Or rather who had it—and then lost it.

"George H. W. Bush used to talk about 'Big Mo,' because they were telling him in meetings, 'You have momentum,'" Carville said just minutes into our conversation. "If you go back and look, he actually is one of the few politicians I've ever known to address it on somewhat of a regular basis."

Indeed, President Bush did have periods of high momentum, curtailed in part by none other than Carville himself.

How did Carville and Governor Bill Clinton's 1992 presidential campaign team engineer a win against an incumbent president who had been enjoying unfathomably high approval ratings—in the 90 percents—just a year before? To those who have come to know Carville's style and approach, few would be surprised that it began with words. Really, with three short sentences:

1. Change versus more of the same.

2. The economy, stupid.

3. Don't forget health care.

The second on this list—"the economy, stupid"—would become particularly salient, finding its way onto billboards, buttons, shirts, mugs, whiteboards, television commercials, radio ads, book covers, cartoon strips, debate stages, and . . . well, everywhere. Thirty years later, Carville's catchphrase would spiral into its own set of memes, each with its own author-generated "it's the fill-in-the-blank, stupid" content.

But the line didn't start off as a public-facing slogan. Rather, Carville wrote these three statements as an internal memo, hung within Clinton's Little Rock headquarters, to help keep staff on message. It was the campaign team's private playbook, so to speak—a set of points to which every member of the organization would agree, and advance around.

It worked. The cohesive message of Clinton's campaign surged, as things do when an organization finds its internal flow.

"It just starts to cascade," Carville told us.

· · ·

Before going further, let's take a step back and look at how the political stage differs from other forms of competition, or in what ways it's alike.

It helps to think of politics as a team sport, which isn't hard to do—it's clear that around each candidate is a campaign structure, and around that campaign are organizations that are to varying degrees aligned: national political parties and the local branches of it, advocacy groups, groups of voters who align on specific issues, donors, and so on.

While the inclination might be to think of the candidate as the quarterback or CEO of a campaign organization, that's not necessarily the most accurate parallel to make. Perhaps in local elections or early in an election cycle, a candidate does fill that role—but at the level of presidential politics, the candidate is one (albeit very important) piece of a much larger machine. In some sense, the candidate may be more like the mascot—an object that symbolizes a team, advances down a field, carries nearly all of the ultimate responsibility, and captures the full attention of bystanders while a world of action just outside the lens buoys each play.

It's also helpful to acknowledge that the organizations surrounding a political campaign are far less, well, organized than a military unit or an actual sports team. Presidential campaigns have multiple managers directing operations across every state, with field teams comprising paid staff and volunteers alike, and there's a lot less control at that level. These operations are surrounded by, and influenced by, the preferences of interest groups and donors, often with competing motivations or policy objectives. There are significant inputs, and it's not always perfectly hierarchical.

Further, while forward motion is quite clear on a sports field, advancement in politics isn't always so certain. In part, this is because the ability to measure "momentum" in politics—short of results on Election Day itself—relies on imperfect tools: instruments such as public opinion polls, attendance counts at rallies, and donations. These are indicators of success, but none on their own are perfect predictors of it.

This is because success in national politics depends on not just the attitudes and feelings of individual actors but upon their behaviors too. A campaign team can operate with extraordinary unity, flow, and responsiveness—can be prepared, focused, and tuned into one another—and yet if people aren't moved to independent action, in the form of casting a ballot, the campaign's objective fails.

This means that the work of political consultants depends considerably on instinct, intuition, and motivation—the very characteristics that led James Carville to rise to the top as he did.

From his perspective today, Carville's view includes many successes beyond his own.

"One of the great momentums was Joe Biden in 2020," Carville offered, describing the Democratic primary. "He ran terribly in Iowa and New Hampshire, ran a little better in Nevada, and then he goes to South Carolina and blows it out, and everybody collectively said, 'Fuck, this thing is over.' Then he just swamped in Virginia and every other place. So he went from zero to sixty in a time like twenty-four seconds, twenty-three seconds, and then two seconds. That was caused by voters validating him."

Carville outlined how "the suburban women in Virginia saw what the Blacks in South Carolina were voting, and they said, 'Okay, this is our guy.' As soon as they saw that everybody was fine for voting for him overwhelmingly, that entire party changed its mind."

It's not surprising, perhaps, that Carville's recent experience of momentum happened at the level of primary elections. That's really where the action falls, Carville believes, at least when it comes to the dynamics of influencing larger portions of the electorate.

"In general elections, we're so polarized. You just don't have that many available voters to change minds as you do in the primaries," he said.

To Carville, validation by other voters is a key ingredient in political momentum—voters seeing how others respond to a candidate and thinking, "Well, they think he's okay; then I think he or she's okay."

And that's what seemed to happen for Joe Biden in South Carolina. His campaign, at that point, was floundering. He hadn't performed well in early primary states and was closing up storefronts in California because the campaign didn't have any money.

"They didn't have any capital," Carville said. "It was nothing until Jim Clyburn stepped in. I've never seen anything like it. They didn't have headquarters. They didn't have anything. They were just rambling around South Carolina, and the Thursday before he just dropped the hammer."

Carville didn't exaggerate. House Majority Whip Jim Clyburn, the highest-ranking African American Democrat in Congress, single-handedly turned the tide for the former vice president's campaign when gifting his endorsement to Biden just days before South Carolina's Democratic primary. Biden's political career was on life support everywhere, South Carolina included. His lead in the polls was in the single digits, and opponents, including billionaire Tom Steyer and Bernie Sanders, were making sizable gains. Clyburn saw this, telling CNN that polls generally "tighten up when you get close to an election." Every candidate in the race wanted Clyburn's endorsement, but Biden got it.

"Once he did that—acceleration. Entirely. Understand—he won the [South Carolina] primary by 63 percent of all the votes from then on," Carville said. "It was Black voters, suburban voters, it was everything. And it did not matter. Once that night came, it was over for. It was just over in an instant. I mean, it was really remarkable."

The cascade that followed was momentous. Biden's decisive victory in South Carolina led multiple moderate opponents to drop out of the race, including Pete Buttigieg and Amy Klobuchar. And in what felt like a clear chain reaction, various other coveted endorsements, such as from Senate Democratic leader Harry Reid, Barack Obama's US ambassador to the UN Susan Rice, and former candidate Beto O'Rourke, all fell to Biden.

The validation from South Carolina voters meant more, it seems, than high-profile endorsements. "That victory seems to have set off a domino effect of support among Democratic voters in southern states and minorities. In the 14 primary contests on Tuesday, Biden won every southern state. According to exit polling, Biden's victories in some of these key states were largely thanks to strong support among minority voters," wrote Daniel Strauss for *The Guardian* on March 4, 2020.

The last remaining moderate Democrat in the race, Michael Bloomberg, soon also left the race, giving Biden his endorsement. There's no doubt that Jim Clyburn lit a match for the Biden campaign. A spark. But if there hadn't been kindling there to fuel and sustain a fire, the results would have been short-lived. There must have been something beneath the surface of Biden's operation that was ready, prepared for momentum.

P olitical momentum is often focused on candidates, issue politics. But the organizations behind social change face similar dynamics.

Over the past few decades, marijuana access in the United States has undergone a remarkable transformation. What began as limited allowances for medical use or low-THC products in a few states has grown into a nationwide shift, with more than two-thirds of states now permitting medical marijuana use and nearly half allowing recreational use. As of 2024, twenty-three states have legalized adult recreational marijuana, representing a significant expansion from just two states, Colorado and Washington, that pioneered recreational legalization in 2012. This rapid change reflects evolving public attitudes, growing acceptance of cannabis for both therapeutic and recreational purposes, and the increasing recognition of its economic potential. The expansion has raised important questions about regulation, public health, and the social impact of legalization, setting the stage for a future where marijuana could be federally legalized.

This shift, while it may look organic from afar, was very much the result of a concerted effort toward change. Research by our friend, health policy consultant Tamara Demko, provided us a unique look into how advocates in one state, Florida, prepared for and achieved a transformational shift in cannabis policy.

In the years leading up to the passage of Florida's 2014 medical cannabis legislation (SB 1030), marijuana reform advocates worked— sometimes diligently, sometimes in disarray—to prepare for a moment of opportunity. Trial and error was matched with tenacity, and over time, cannabis advocates laid an effective groundwork based on strong leadership and strategic communications that positioned the issue as ready for a "spark" when it arrived.

Demko, a Harvard-educated health policy attorney and registered nurse, holds a PhD in public health and had a front-row seat to how this unfolded, both as a professional within Florida's political process and in her academic research that included extensive informant interviews, surveys, literature reviews, and data analysis.

"Prior to 2014, there was no shortage of efforts to open up Florida's then highly restrictive marijuana laws, but roadblocks appeared at every turn," she told us. "Marijuana reform advocates had long observed that public opinion on medical cannabis was shifting, both nationally and within Florida, but there was no clear path forward for legitimate policy reform."

In response, advocates began to organize, building from loose coalitions of like-minded people and organizations into more structured entities. They recognized that the first step toward big change would likely be seen in the form of incremental progress and began to focus on alliances with sympathetic stakeholders and proponents of medical cannabis—particularly for the treatment of serious illnesses like epilepsy—which promised broader appeal. They recruited lawmakers—key legislative champions—who could shepherd the issue through the state's political machinery.

While in business, sports, and the military, it's leaders (CEOs, coaches, officers) who recruit team members, in political efforts, it's often the opposite. In politics, advocacy groups and other coalitions have to recruit leaders—bill sponsors, legislative allies, and even political candidates—to carry their issues.

"In Florida, the medical marijuana movement had to find the right people, the key legislative champions, who could shepherd the issue through the state's political machinery," Demko shared. These leaders had to be not only from the party that was in control but from key districts within the state, with strong relationships not only within the legislature but with the executive branch too. After all, no legislature in the United States is immune from executive veto, and even highly successful legislative efforts run this risk.

"Strong leadership was essential in driving this momentum forward," Demko explained. "Key figures in the movement, including legislators from both parties, took up the cause. Republican legislators like Senator Rob Bradley and Representative Matt Gaetz, both prominent figures in Florida's conservative political sphere, emerged as champions of the medical cannabis bill. Their sponsorship of SB 1030 was instrumental in moving the bill forward, as their leadership reassured more hesitant members of the legislature that the bill was both politically viable and morally sound."

With leaders identified, targeted communication began with different stakeholders, including with legislators, health care professionals, and the public. Public opinion polling, some of which included message-testing experiments, provided feedback to advocates about which types of narratives worked, and which didn't, in persuading anti-marijuana voters to change their minds. Through this type of feedback and more, advocates framed the issue as one of compassion, highlighting cases like that of Charlotte Figi, a child with epilepsy whose seizures were alleviated by a strain of low-THC cannabis. This narrative was essential in generating empathy and reducing opposition, as it reframed the conversation away from recreational marijuana and toward the health and well-being of vulnerable children.

The true turning point for marijuana reform in Florida came in 2014, when a constitutional amendment on medical marijuana was proposed for the November ballot. This amendment, if passed, had the potential to reshape Florida's political landscape, particularly by mobilizing Democratic voters in what was expected to be a tight gubernatorial race. Republican lawmakers, concerned about the potential electoral impact, saw the passage of SB 1030 as a way to address the growing demand for medical cannabis reform while maintaining control over the issue.

Advocates were prepared for this moment. They had already laid the groundwork with legislative champions, built coalitions, and framed their message in a way that resonated with both the public and policymakers. When the threat of the constitutional amendment emerged, they were able to leverage this political urgency to advance their bill. By positioning SB 1030 as a more controlled, narrowly focused alternative to the broader constitutional amendment, advocates were able to convince lawmakers that passing their bill was the best way to retain legislative control over the issue while addressing public demand.

The CNN documentary featuring Charlotte Figi provided the emotional spark that advocates needed to push their cause over the line. The story of a young girl whose life had been dramatically improved by medical cannabis resonated deeply with the public and legislators alike. Advocates quickly capitalized on this media attention, using it to reinforce their message of compassion and urgency. This public narrative helped overcome opposition by shifting the focus away from drug users and toward innocent children in need of medical help.

The combination of strategic framing, strong leadership, and timely advocacy allowed marijuana reform advocates to use the constitutional amendment and media attention as catalysts for their own legislative success. Their careful preparation meant that when the political landscape shifted in their favor, they were ready to act. They mobilized their networks, lobbied legislators with renewed urgency, and highlighted the growing public support for medical cannabis. In doing so, they successfully steered SB 1030 through the legislative process, culminating in its passage just as the 2014 session came to a close.

The passage of SB 1030 underscores the importance of preparation in advocacy. Advocates had anticipated the moment when medical cannabis would become a politically viable issue, and they had recruited the right leaders and built the relationships, narratives, and coalitions necessary to act when the opportunity arose. Their readiness allowed them to capitalize on the momentum created by external factors—such as the proposed constitutional amendment and media attention—while maintaining control over the direction of the reform.

"This case study demonstrates that effective advocacy is not only about responding to political shifts but about creating the conditions that make those shifts possible," Demko said. "Marijuana reform advocates in Florida were able to turn a political spark into legislative success because they had built a solid foundation long before the spark arrived. Their preparation ensured that when the opportunity for momentum came, they were not only ready but positioned to ride the wave and lead the charge."

In the end, the passage of SB 1030 was not just about seizing the moment; it was about being ready for the moment to arrive. This readiness turned a potential threat—the constitutional amendment—into a strategic advantage and allowed advocates to achieve a legislative victory that had eluded them in previous years.

The spark turned into a slow burn. Soon after Florida approved the use of low-THC medical marijuana, the state expanded access to other THC varieties as well, albeit through physician recommendations.

"It *should* be like that," Jensen Huang told *60 Minutes* in May 2024 after hearing how employees at his company, Nvidia, described the company's culture and, more specifically, Huang's leadership style as a "demanding perfectionist" who "isn't easy to work for." The sixty-one-year-old CEO, who went from a "relentlessly bullied" teen washing dishes and bathrooms at diners to the thirteenth-richest person in the world with a net worth greater than $100 billion, runs his company much like the machines his company builds. Where most CEOs have about ten direct reports, Huang has fifty. Like General

Petraeus walking patrols with his units, something few of his rank would do, Huang sees this structure as essential to avoiding unnecessary layers of management that can hinder transparency and slow progress. His tenure at Nvidia is also disproportionate to other Silicon Valley CEOs—three decades at the helm—and attrition at Nvidia among its workers is also unusually low despite their having ample opportunities to bring their skills elsewhere.

Somehow, despite having about five times the number of direct reports that other major CEOs have, Huang has been criticized for lacking a personal touch with his employees. But Huang wasn't the only leader, and Nvidia's story wasn't his alone.

In this book, we've thought about leaders primarily as a single person at the top of a team or unit—and surely, many leaders operate with autonomy or in a hierarchy with few on the top. But the team that started Nvidia looked different and started even more differently. The entire early operation ran out of a small condo without A/C, with a team structure that was as flat as the space itself. There was no sprawling org chart, no layers of middle management—just three visionary leaders dividing the responsibility among themselves, each contributing their unique strengths to push the fledgling company forward.

Huang, the dynamic and ambitious CEO, was the driving force of the company. His role was not only to guide the strategic direction but to keep the company aligned with an audacious vision: to become the most important technology company in the world. While Huang may not have been deeply involved in the technical minutiae at first, he understood technology at a fundamental level and had an unparalleled knack for understanding how business and technology could intersect. In many ways, Huang was the external face of Nvidia, the person who could sell their ideas and their future.

Chris Malachowsky, the engineer, was the one who could build just about anything. In the early organization, Malachowsky was responsible for bringing Nvidia's ideas to life. He focused on solving the complex technical problems that came with creating cutting-edge graphics technology in a time when the industry itself was still in its infancy. His role was hands-on and deeply technical; he was the one who ensured that Nvidia's innovations were more than just concepts—they worked.

Then there was Curtis Priem, the systems architect. Priem was the mastermind behind the overall design, able to look at the full scope of what Nvidia was trying to accomplish and find solutions that others couldn't see. He filled in the gaps between Malachowsky's engineering and Huang's grand vision, ensuring the technology could function seamlessly and with long-term potential. While Malachowsky could build it, Priem was the one who figured out what "it" needed to be, translating the company's goals into a product that could change industries.

Together, these three founders formed the first and only true "org chart" at Nvidia. There were no rigid roles—each one contributed to the business in ways that often overlapped, their collective focus being survival and eventual success. And even as their beginning suffered no bureaucratic red tape, the three were preparing for growth.

But how?

Sitting down to talk with Chris Malachowsky was a rare, treasured opportunity for a personal glimpse into how this trio grew to what Nvidia has become and how they prepared for the spark that drove the company's meteoric rise, and Malachowsky was generous with his time.

"I think this is quite unique among startups: We had the objective of being the most important technology company in the world," Malachowsky shared. "We were three guys in an un-air-conditioned condominium, yet we had that objective. This is not trying to be self-serving, but we were independently exceptional at what we were doing. I was the engineer. I felt I could build anything and welcomed Curtis defining for us what was needed. Curtis could figure out anything from soup to nuts, and then tell you, 'In the middle we need a saucepan.' And then Jensen was just this brilliant technologist who had all the people skills. Independently we could go do our thing."

O nly video gamers had really heard of Nvidia in its early years, after its first product launched in 1995. It was video game enthusiasts, PC manufacturers, and arcade machine developers who became familiar with the brand first—drawn in by its innovative multimedia accelerator card. But its widespread use was limited by major compatibility issues with existing software. In 1999, Nvidia introduced the GeForce 256, marketed as the world's first GPU (graphics processing unit). We all rely on GPUs, which are specialized electronic circuits designed to accelerate the creation and rendering of images, videos, and animations and that handle the complex calculations required to produce high-quality graphics. GPUs are essential components in modern computing, particularly for applications requiring intensive visual processing—intricate technology that most people take for granted but have no real concept of their workings.

Needless to say, GPUs were a significant advancement in graphics technology, establishing Nvidia's products as superior in performance and capabilities compared to competitors. Many would have thought that this would be enough—dominating the expanding demand for graphics cards in an already booming gaming market. But Nvidia's leadership saw even greater applications for its technologies.

The GPU processes complex mathematical calculations to transform 2D and 3D data into images that can be displayed on a screen. This involves tasks like shading, texture mapping, and polygon rendering. Unlike CPUs, which are designed for serial processing, GPUs excel at parallel processing. This means they can handle thousands of operations simultaneously, making them ideal for graphics rendering and other data-intensive tasks. Scientific simulations and data analysis benefit from the ability to perform many calculations simultaneously, speeding up research and development.

It was clear to Huang, Malachowsky, and Priem that the GPU could be transformative in the areas of engineering and modeling, big data, medical breakthroughs, and artificial intelligence. The parallel processing power of GPUs makes them ideal for machine learning and training deep neural networks, which require massive computational resources to handle large datasets and complex calculations.

You may recall the concept of "potential energy" from high school physics: stored energy that is held until a point of release. Think of a spring that's stretched, a match that's not yet struck, or a ball that's at the apex of a hill—not yet in motion but, when triggered, a significant display of energy is apparent. In other words, potential energy is not a characteristic of an individual entity but rather is a property of a system. It arises within organizations based on how various parts exert forces on one another: gravity, with the earth, or chemical elements that when mixed undergo mutual changes in composition.

In the case of Nvidia, potential energy was building through quiet, patient, relentless research. In 2013, Nvidia spent more than one quarter of its revenue on R&D, far outpacing its largest competitor, Intel, and 80 percent more than the industry average. They were investing as they prepared for moments ahead. Samsung, for example, spent only 8.2 percent of its revenues on R&D in 2013, and Toshiba, 17.1 percent.

It was an employee within the ranks that first observed the potential for AI. One of Malachowsky's researchers, Bryan Cantanzaro, had done some seminal work in early AI and brought some ideas to the team. "At that point, I was running our advanced research group," Malachowsky said. "One of the things about Jensen's leadership and our executives is that we respect the fact that there's lots of great people and they have lots of great ideas, and we should culturally encourage their passion to pursue the best of their ideas, you know, support them, let them flesh things out." He likened this approach to the concept of an incubator, where innovation can happen within the walls, and one doesn't have to leave a company to try something new.

"There's a lot of that," he continued. "We always paid attention to when these brilliant people had a very strong feeling behind something. Bryan clearly felt AI was a big deal. Jensen latched onto it, learned a whole bunch about it. These were the brilliant guys that helped move the needle and bring this out of academia and research labs into the light of day and started the AI revolution." Huang narrowed in on the opportunity, Malachowsky said, and pivoted Nvidia to be uniquely positioned for it. They didn't wait for the market to dictate their path but leveraged their parallel computing capabilities to focus on AI's potential. Nvidia's researchers recognized that its GPUs—originally designed for rendering graphics—were also well suited for the parallel processing required in AI and deep learning. They set out to develop processing power strong and nimble enough to serve the complex needs of AI partners and deep learning tasks.

While those competitors were already household names, and might have seen reports of Nvidia's research investments, they were probably not too fazed by what it meant. What may have seemed like desperation or delusion was in fact Nvidia's measured preparation, laying the groundwork for projects destined to stay under wraps for almost a decade. Competitors had no idea that Nvidia's R&D efforts were not just about enhancing their GPUs for gaming—a market they already dominated—but also delving into AI, autonomous vehicles, and deep learning. Its strategy was patience: wait for the perfect market conditions before unveiling groundbreaking technologies.

Long before the "AI boom" took hold in the popular marketplace, these projects were quietly advancing at a rapid pace at Nvidia. Their engineers and scientists were pushing the boundaries of what their technology could achieve, setting the stage for a future where their innovations would revolutionize multiple industries. In other words, Nvidia was not merely reacting to current market demands; it was preparing for future shifts, ensuring that when the right moment arrived, they would be ready to lead the charge with cutting-edge technology that would fill a need its consumers would be just coming to realize they wanted fulfilled.

Nvidia continued to prepare, continued to recruit the best minds and stay as flat as possible to ensure the ability to pivot. Nvidia wasn't preparing for a great quarter or a new contract. They were preparing for a spark.

Editor's Note

As this book was going to press, the investment world that had pushed Nvidia to become one the world's three most valuable companies received shocking news. A Chinese company called DeepSeek claimed that it had built an AI open-source, large language model called R1 that was comparable to OpenAI's ChatGPT. But DeepSeek said it had done so for only $6 million, a tiny fraction of what big Nvidia clients were spending on these models. Overnight, Nvidia stock dropped by 17 percent and the company lost $600 billion in value, the largest one-day drop for a single company in the market's history. Some pundits declared the DeepSeek announcement as the "end of Nvidia." Some believed that the spark behind Nvidia has been doused.

The only people that didn't panic were Jensen Huang and his team. They knew that it was a less-advanced version of their own product that had allowed the Chinese company to build the model. And they had long prepared for the idea that cheaper alternatives would rise. Huang was silent for the first few days but ultimately offered a response, saying investors "got it wrong" and that the advent of products like DeepSeek's would only add fuel to the world's desire for more AI models. Huang said: "It is so incredibly exciting. The energy around the world as a result of R1 becoming open-sourced—incredible." And Huang made it clear that several significant products to fuel AI growth were in development at Nvidia.

It didn't take long for Wall Street to hear and believe Nvidia's message. The company recovered nearly all the value lost in a matter of weeks.

T he *Oxford English Dictionary* defines *preparation* as "the action or process of making ready or being made ready for use or consideration." It is important to distinguish between the actions taken to accomplish the mission and those taken to prepare for executing those actions.

ACTION 1:
Focus primarily on building task cohesion.

Task cohesion refers to how well a team can work together in order to achieve common goals, tasks, or achievements (Schneider, Gruman, & Coutts, 2012). Conversely, social cohesion refers to the degree to which members of a team like each other and interact accordingly (Richardson, 2013). Research indicates that the influence between the different forms of cohesion is bidirectional. But task cohesion has a stronger influence on social cohesion rather than the other way around. The implication of the relationship is that leaders are well advised to lean into learning what it takes to collectively perform the work well more so than primarily focusing on building strong bonds first.

ACTION 2:
Create realistic experiences to set the conditions for how you will "meet the moment."

The military has a saying: "Train as you will fight." The adage informs a philosophy of creating training scenarios that replicate combat conditions to prepare soldiers for the stress of those environments. Such scenarios (for example, special teams, two-minute drills, red zone offense, soccer placekicks) are routinely integrated into practice and executed with precision on sports teams. Leaders in all fields must routinely take their people through experiences that will help them to seize sparks (or reverse them) when they occur.

ACTION 3:
Develop your team's ability to take smart risks.

Dynamic environments routinely reveal gaps in understanding or capabilities. To seize momentum, teams must frequently take risks. Encourage your team to evaluate the potential consequences of taking risks so they can make an informed decision about whether or not to proceed with them. Smart risks are ones that can propel something forward if navigated well and can be absorbed if success is not achieved. Conversely, dumb risks are ones where there is no coming back from falling short of the objective. Great organizations routinely underwrite smart risk and never underwrite dumb risk.

8

Spark

While Nvidia's research teams were making major, albeit quiet, moves designing processors that would be uniquely powerful for the needs of AI and deep learning, there was a new company out there looking for just that. OpenAI was founded in 2015 with the goal of advancing AI in a way that benefits humanity, and they quickly realized that the computational demands for training large AI models were immense. OpenAI, from the outset, needed highly scalable computational power to achieve its ambitious goals, and Nvidia's GPUs were the natural choice—few alternatives could match Nvidia's hardware capabilities for AI training. OpenAI's AI models grew in complexity and turned increasingly to Nvidia's GPUs for their unmatched performance in processing the massive datasets required for training.

The results of Nvidia's preparation emerged in a whirlwind almost a decade later when ChatGPT propelled into the public view and demand for Nvidia's GPUs and other chips skyrocketed in turn. Within two months of release, ChatGPT gathered a hundred million users, the fastest adoption of any platform in history. In 2019, Nvidia's market value was around $100 billion. From the launch of ChatGPT to March 12, 2024, Nvidia's stock price increased by 428 percent. By mid-2023, Nvidia's valuation had surpassed $1 trillion for the first time. As of this writing, its value has exceeded $3 trillion, making Nvidia one of just three companies to boast such a value.

ChatGPT—the spark to Nvidia's preparation—set in motion a fire that's still burning.

To some observers, the explosion of products from Nvidia since 2022 is evidence that the company had developed innovations and brought them to market very, very fast. But what looked to observers like sudden momentum was in fact the result of intentional, and tedious, preparation. Huang and Malachowsky, the archers who had pulled a full sheaf of arrows further and further back in their company's bow, set in motion a display of momentum few other companies will ever experience. Nvidia's momentum may have appeared sudden to those watching the market but in fact was built through years of intensive research and strategic patience, which catapulted them to the forefront of technological advancement.

The spark (massive public adoption of AI products) would never alone catapult Nvidia into the force it is today. Other elements of our Momentum Model had laid the groundwork. For example, Huang's leadership demanded a culture where senior executives are expected to operate independently, work relentlessly, and take aim for the mark. And, Malachowsky shared with us, Nvidia had a concrete, intentional approach to recruitment. Malachowsky shared a lesson that may be uncomfortable for other teams to replicate: If they didn't find the right talent, they didn't hire at all.

"We committed ourselves that we were just going to hire the best, that we're not going to bring on the mediocre. We're just going to wait it out. Maybe be understaffed, but we're going to hire the best," he explained. "We've got a workforce that's not put off by being undermanned. I actually think it's a badge of strength. I think depravity may not be the right term, but being in a state of want is clarifying, and it makes you be thoughtful and, you know, helps you, helps you strategize."

Nvidia's founders also recognized that their business was prone to ups and downs in workload. Malachowsky shared that in the world of semiconductors, there was no success story that lasted more than a season or two. "We wanted to weather that," he said. "And so we'd hire a rocket scientist and ask him to sweep the floor. I'd rather have him do that than somebody whose only capacity was to do that, because tomorrow, the shit is going to hit the fan, and we're going to ask you to go back to rocket science." In other words, Malachowsky said, "I wanted to give you credit for the fact that I've underutilized you for the benefit of a future that I haven't yet seen."

Once Nvidia recruited the right people, the emphasis focused on fulfilling obligations to those already on board and fostering a positive team climate. "You've got to do them justice and give them the opportunity to succeed," Malachowsky said. "We want to hire smart people and then listen to them. You surround them with great people. We tell our managers, 'You want to be the dumbest one in the room.' That is exciting. That is motivating."

Even as Nvidia grew, the org structure remained as flat as possible—a feature many credit for its extraordinary rise and sustained momentum. The three founders were comfortable with an all-hands-on-deck approach where people could be pulled from one area to another depending on where the greatest needs were at that moment. This gave Nvidia an atypical ability to pivot.

"I know it's a little passé, but I used to tell the people that work for me, somebody comes to you and asks for your help on something that's a priority, you go do it; tell me about it later. I don't care. Go do the right thing; fill us in later," Malachowsky said, explaining a process that few managers would find themselves comfortable offering. "HR was the last one to generally know how people were spending their time. You know, even your manager may not know exactly. You know whatever you're doing. We're not asking you to ask for permission. Let us pull you back later if you made a wrong choice, but pivot quickly. Get, get on things. Don't be hung up."

The ability to pivot is perhaps of greatest benefit, however, when it's coupled with a strong intuition for noticing opportunities when they arise. The leaders of Nvidia saw the spark in OpenAI and had in place its own unique but tested approach to leadership, culture, recruitment, and preparation.

M omentum, by its very definition, requires a moment. Something happens that begins moving things, preferably in your direction. We've chosen to call that moment your "spark."

Sometimes the spark is obvious: the announcement of a game-changing technology that you are uniquely positioned to help grow (like ChatGPT); the fumble that you turn into a touchdown (as the Patriots did in the 2017 Super Bowl); or the unexpected endorsement in a political campaign (as happened when Representative Clyburn put his arm around a floundering Joe Biden during the 2020 Democratic presidential primary). Sometimes the spark has a slow burn to it: the hiring of the right coach or leader who makes moves that quietly add up to a changed atmosphere, or the addition of a few courageous voices to a movement that speaks out against sexual harassment.

Ultimately, the spark is the place where belief systems begin to shift. Momentum is a mentality. It's as much about your belief system as it is about the outcomes. One of the keys to this block in the model is how leaders train their team to see the spark. You want the team to see it favorably, though that doesn't always happen naturally. Some on a team might see a spark and react, "If this happens, it will mean so much more work for us." But when the leader can help frame it favorably, the team should think, "Look at all the opportunities we should get!"

To do this well requires the ability to see the spark when it appears and to help fan it in a way that the flame of momentum becomes unstoppable.

Leaders can prepare their teams to recognize a spark in a variety of ways. Here are three examples of preparatory activities. First, they must strive to ensure clarity exists within the team regarding the organizational objectives and potential outcomes associated with them. There is research that concluded work performance was enhanced when process and goal clarity was high provided that team members are committed to the goal.

Second, leaders must share information effectively to prepare their teams for seizing opportunities. Information power is one of the six power bases defined by John R. P. French and Bertram Raven in "The Bases of Social Power." This type of power is focused on the ability to control the flow of information required to get things done. Information power is one of the three bases that if utilized well is likely to lead to greater commitment. (Altogether, there are six power bases that are likely to bring out one of three outcomes: commitment, compliance, or resistance.)

Finally, leaders must teach their teams to collaborate. Numerous research studies have detailed how organizations benefit from effective collaboration. The 2007 *Harvard Business Review* article "Eight Ways to Build Collaborative Teams" by Lynda Gratton and Tamara J. Erickson detailed the following preparatory actions leaders should continually strengthen in order to enhance collaboration: investing in signature relationship practices (for example, securing state-of-the-art team collaboration software); senior leaders modeling collaborative behaviors; creating a "gift" culture (that is, mentoring and coaching people regularly at all levels); ensuring the requisite skills (for example, equipping employees through training to understand they can build relationships, communicate well, and resolve conflicts creatively); supporting a strong sense of community; assigning team leaders that are task and relationship oriented; building on "heritage" relationships (that is, placing at least a few people who have worked together previously on the team); and making sure individual roles are clearly defined and the team is empowered to figure out how to accomplish its tasks.

S uccess can provide a spark, but so, too, can tragedy. It's often uncomfortable to talk about, and we have certainly struggled with how to portray stories of positive momentum that started with a terrible event. Not every disaster results in momentum toward positive change. But this does happen, and it represents a type of spark that— discomforts and all—shouldn't be discounted.

In politics and public policy, this potential is not uncommon: The spark for social change is often delivered from a particularly egregious wrongdoing or oversight. Public policy, at its best, predicts its own flaws and adjusts before calamity strikes, but in reality, policy change takes enormous effort and doesn't abide by any set schedule. Sometimes, advocates for a certain issue feel like they're screaming into a black hole, hoping their voices will result in heightened awareness of a problem; and sometimes, these voices go unheard until something terrible happens. The illustration we chose here is especially dramatic, both in the magnitude of catastrophe that represented the spark but also in the immediacy of change it led to. It also happens to be devastatingly literal.

• • •

On Saturday, March 25, 1911, the workday at the Triangle Shirtwaist Factory in New York City was winding down. The hum of sewing machines filled the air as the afternoon sun streamed through the grimy windows. The factory, located on the top three floors of the Asch Building in New York City, was a maze of narrow aisles crammed with rows of tables, fabric scraps, and about five hundred young women—mostly immigrants and some as young as fourteen—hunched over their work.

The fire that took hold and rapidly consumed the building is believed to have started from a discarded cigarette or match igniting a bin of cotton scraps. Within minutes of the spark—whatever it had been—flames spread rapidly through the factory, feeding on the fabric and paper patterns scattered everywhere. The workers were thrown into panic. They rushed toward the exits, but escape was hindered by several factors, including the cruel but common practice by factory owners to lock doors and stairwells in order to avoid theft and unauthorized breaks from work. The factory was a death trap.

Yetta Lubitz, a survivor of the fire, later testified about the harrowing experience. She described the chaos and desperation that engulfed the factory floor. There was no time to think, she recounted—the smoke was suffocating, and the women could hardly see through it. With the main exit blocked, workers sought other ways out. Some tried to use the fire escape, but the flimsy structure collapsed under the weight of the fleeing workers, sending many plummeting to their deaths. Others, in a desperate bid to escape the flames, jumped from the windows, only to meet a tragic end on the pavement below. Some, such as Yetta, managed to survive by fleeing to the roof, where they were rescued by neighboring buildings' employees who helped them to safety. Firefighters arrived quickly, but their equipment was inadequate. Their ladders could reach only the sixth floor, far below the burning factory floors. Witnesses on the street watched in horror as the fire consumed the building and workers jumped to their deaths.

In the aftermath, 146 workers were confirmed dead. The public outrage that followed the fire was immense. It sparked a wave of mourning and anger that swept through the city. Vigils and protests were held, demanding justice for the lives lost. The tragedy exposed the brutal realities of industrial labor and ignited a movement for change, and indeed, it electrified existing efforts to improve working conditions.

One witness to the fire was Frances Perkins. She was having tea with friends nearby when she heard the commotion and rushed to the scene. She saw the horrors of workers jumping from the burning building and suffocating inside. Perkins was no stranger to the need for reform. She was already deeply involved in labor advocacy—working with organizations like the New York Consumers League, which aimed to improve labor conditions, particularly for women and children. She had already been advocating for reforms to working hours, safer conditions, and better wages when she witnessed, before her eyes, perhaps the most tragic justification for her concerns. Her involvement only increased from there—she was appointed to the Committee on Safety of the City of New York and ultimately was appointed as the first female US secretary of labor by President Franklin D. Roosevelt.

"The fire at the Triangle Factory was the day the New Deal began," Perkins later recalled. The New York State Legislature created the Factory Investigating Commission, which resulted in more than thirty new laws regulating labor conditions that went well beyond fire safety and into areas modern workers can rely on protections for—working hours, building inspections, sanitation, and more. The fire and the subsequent reforms laid the groundwork for future labor movements, including the establishment of the Occupational Safety and Health Administration in 1970.

To many—including some history books—it would seem that the Triangle Shirtwaist Factory Fire was singularly responsible for the outcry and subsequent legislative changes that came. But organized efforts for worker protections were long underway. The International Ladies' Garment Workers' Union was founded in 1900 and had already organized massive efforts, including a twenty-thousand-strong strike in 1909; and the Women's Trade Union League, founded in 1903, was active in supporting such efforts including through providing bail for arrested strikers and organizers. The factory fire drew attention to the need for such efforts—galvanizing many more to join and propelling momentum for a movement whose leadership was prepared to advocate in the aftermath of tragedy.

O nce humankind grasped it could create and control fire, man's reliance on this element profoundly changed everything from basic survival, diet and culture, technology, and even evolution. Fire offered warmth in cold climates, protection from predators, and a means to cook food, which made nutrients easier to digest and less likely to carry disease. Fire also extended human activities into the night, fostering social interactions and lending to the development of language and storytelling. Campfires, to this day, have that effect. Archaeological evidence reveals a variety of techniques used by early humans to start fires. The earliest known method was likely the use of natural fire sources, such as lightning strikes—capturing the fire from brush fires or even embers from lava flows and taking great measures to preserve the energy. But humans soon developed their own techniques for fire-making too. One of the oldest methods is the friction-based fire-starting technique, exemplified by the hand drill and the bow drill. Another method, the fire plow, involves rubbing a wooden stick against a groove in a fireboard to produce hot dust that ignites. Percussion methods, such as striking flint against pyrite or steel, were also used.

Today, most take fire for granted. But if asked to start one from scratch, most would also fail. The same, only more so, is true with what it takes to ignite momentum—unlike physical fires, the sparks that ignite momentum may not be easy to spot. And beyond that, without human observation or perception, these momentum-igniting sparks may not exist at all.

"If a tree falls in the forest and nobody is there to hear it, does it make a sound?" This thought experiment raises questions about observation, reality, and physics itself. From a scientific perspective, sound is a mechanical wave that results from the vibration of particles in a medium such as air, water, or solids. When a tree falls, it creates vibrations in the air that propagate as sound waves. Therefore, scientifically, the tree falling must, and does, produce sound waves regardless of whether anyone is present to hear them. But to Irish philosopher George Berkeley, who posed this question in the eighteenth century, the question is really a deeper one that delves into the nature of perception and reality. To Berkeley, this musing cut to the heart of subjective idealism—the idea that reality exists only as it is perceived by the mind. Berkeley argued that for something to exist, it must be perceived. In his view, if no one is there to perceive the sound, then it does not exist. This idea emphasizes the role of the observer in the existence of phenomena: Without our consciousness, nothing exists.

In other words, objects or events don't have objective existence outside of human perception.

In few contexts is this concept more true or important than in the existence of sparks that ignite momentum for teams: For the most part, these sparks exist only if someone sees them. The spark—the moment, the opportunity, the flash of lightning or the first faint wisp of smoke—means something only if someone is there to observe it *and* sees it for what it is. Some sparks, or perhaps even many, can be destructive. And sometimes, that destruction—to social norms, a competitor's winning streak, or an enemy's advancement—is desirable to some. But for all of the various types of sparks, when it comes to the potential for initiating momentum, all share the necessity of someone to notice and act upon it. Some groundwork would have been laid for the flame to take hold—through preparation, organization, and an environment readied for the change.

A great leader will amplify the spark by recognizing that true momentum is driven by an event that begins to change the minds and climate for a team that's been preparing to take advantage of it.

Sometimes, spark is huge. And sometimes, it's the result of honest conversations between two leaders intent on making a positive difference.

The Ford Motor Company was losing lots of money in the early 2000s. William (Bill) Clay Ford Jr. had assumed the company's CEO role in October 2001 (in addition to holding the chairman role), and in the five years afterward, the company lost approximately $9.1 billion through July 2006. Bill Ford and the board knew change was required. So they set about finding a leader who could revive the company's fortunes in the beginning of what held the potential to become a global economic downturn.

Bill Ford was fully committed to saving the company and his family legacy. With two major US automakers staring at the possibility of entering bankruptcy, the American auto industry was in dire straits. Consequently, Ford designated three board members (Irvine O. Hockaday, former CEO of Hallmark; John L. Thornton, former president and co-COO of Goldman Sachs Group.; and Jorma Ollila, former chairman and CEO of Nokia) to head up the CEO search committee.

Ultimately, the search committee determined that a strong candidate would have several attributes. The ideal person must have demonstrated an exceptional track record of outstanding accomplishments at the highest levels. Additionally, it was imperative the individual possess extensive experience in complex manufacturing and operations. The ideal candidate would possess a deep understanding of technology (present and emerging) and its relevance to different types of power plants (internal combustion, electric-powered, and hybrid). Finally, the ideal candidate would need to possess exceptional grit and a problem-solving orientation. Ultimately, Thornton recommended the board consider Alan Mulally (the president and CEO of Boeing Commercial Airplanes).

Mulally was a Boeing lifer. He began his career there in 1969 as an aerospace engineer. Throughout the years he had climbed the ranks while working on many of the organization's biggest programs (for example, 727, 737, 747, 757, 767, 777), ultimately becoming commercial airplanes CEO in 2001. Yet he was passed over twice for the Boeing CEO job. Mulally had won multiple awards in the industry while fostering sustained commercial success for his business. He also had a reputation as a humble, resolute, "lead by example" type of individual. Given his track record and attributes, Mulally quickly emerged as the leading candidate for the Ford role.

Bill Ford was so convinced Mulally could be the spark Ford needed that he offered to give up the chairman role if doing so was necessary to lock up a deal. Initially, the board connected with Mulally through a mutual acquaintance (Gordon Bethune, former chairman and CEO of Continental Airlines). But multiple intimate conversations between Ford and Mulally are what cemented the latter's ascension into the CEO role.

Mulally once said, "Leadership is having a compelling vision, a comprehensive plan, relentless implementation and talented people working together." Creating all four of those outcomes is not easy. The Ford Motor Company lost $12.7 billion in 2006 and $30 billion total between 2006 and 2008. Yet it was profitable again by 2009 and had completely revamped its product offerings. The company was also the only major domestic automaker to decline taking the government bailout money (Troubled Asset Relief Program). Mulally's recruitment and leadership helped to revamp the company's culture and changed how they prepared to compete and win. So, how did he do it? Mulally utilized eleven principles to drive beliefs and create a performance culture leveraging effective communications driven by his weekly "business plan review" (BPR).

The BPR involved profit center leaders and the twelve functional area heads. The integration of the BPR into the organization's processes was very difficult initially due to the company's long-standing silos (borne out of a large set of diffuse brands) and reputation for infighting. Furthermore, leaders were not used to highlighting shortcomings in their communications.

Mulally's BPR required each member of the leadership team to brief the status of their major projects (green for "on plan," yellow for requiring attention, and red for urgent situations). All BPR items were connected to operational targets that played a role in fostering profitable growth. Anything that generated, delayed, or cost the company profitable growth was measured and assigned a color-coded status map. But leaders were less than forthcoming when briefing their status for several months after initiating the process. Everyone kept briefing their status as "green" despite the company's well-known shortcomings. Mulally knew he had to build trust, and therefore he demonstrated patience as this subterfuge transpired.

Then, one leader briefed his status as yellow, and an audible gasp was exhaled by the BPR attendees. Mulally's response was simply, "Okay, how can we address the situation?" Mulally then followed up with "I can't fix it on my own but the people on this call can." That moment was the spark that got people to buy into the process, and the rest is history, as they say. Bill Ford's belief in Alan Mulally's competence and character made the spark possible when he took a chance on someone outside the industry whom he trusted to get the job done.

LEADER ACTIONS

When the word *spark* is used as a verb, it means "stimulating a dramatic event or process." Momentum leaders act in service of creating positive sparks that galvanize people's motivation (a force influencing direction, effort, and persistence) to perform actions that advance a team's objectives.

ACTION 1:
Foster clarity by the establishment of a clear mission statement and SMART goals to support its accomplishment.

George T. Doran's SMART goals framework (that is, specific, measurable, attainable, relevant, time bounded) is a vehicle for improving motivation and performance. Leaders must create a mission statement that is cogently understood by all team members. Subsequently, they must craft plans and objectives that support accomplishment of the mission. Ensuring your people can make the linkage between the mission and the spark can enhance their willingness to strengthen pursuit of the SMART goals. Edwin Locke and Gary P. Latham's research highlighted the importance of five components in goal setting (clarity, challenge, acceptance, feedback, complexity), and the leader action we recommend ties directly to clarity and challenge.

ACTION 2:
Enhance the team's ability to collaborate effectively.

A 2017 *Harvard Business Review* research publication cited several reasons why collaboration encounters obstacles. The top three reasons cited were "silos (67%), the lack of collaborative vision from leaders (32%), and senior managers not wanting to give up control (32%)." To address sparks effectively requires coordinated action by teams. Enhancing the team's collaboration acumen is essential if they are to act decisively and effectively when a spark occurs. Patrick Lencioni's *Five Dysfunctions of a Team* identified challenges teams routinely experience when seeking to "grow together." Flipping the five dysfunctions is a recipe for strengthening collaboration: build trust, develop practices for addressing conflict, make team commitments, hold team members accountable for their behavior, and focus on collective results.

ACTION 3:
Create shared understanding.

Information is power. The US Army framework for creating high-performing teams (that is, Mission Command) utilizes "shared understanding" as one of its key principles. Shared understanding is "the ability of multiple people to use common knowledge to achieve shared goals. It's based on the idea that understanding is an ability, and that people can modify their thoughts and actions to achieve their goals." Jessica R. Mesmer-Magnus and Leslie A. DeChurch's meta-analysis published in the *Journal of Applied Psychology* found that information sharing positively predicted team performance, cohesion, knowledge integration, and member satisfaction.

9

Leader
Communications

We like to think leadership is about words. Words that inspire. Words that encourage. Words that direct. Words that bring clarity in the fog of uncertainty. But here's the truth: Leadership communication is rarely about the words you say. It's about the things you *do*.

Think about it. The most powerful leaders don't just talk. They act. They signal with every move they make. Sometimes it's in the heat of the moment, when they step in without saying a word and change the entire trajectory of a situation. Other times, it's a nod, a look, or even silence that says more than any speech ever could. And then there are the moments when the communication is baked into the preparation itself—the hours spent getting ready so that when the time comes, the message is clear without a single word being uttered: *This is what we've trained for.*

Words matter, sure. But actions are the real conversation. They're what separates good leaders from those rare few who spark momentum and turn the tide. Leadership communication is a constant pulse, an unspoken exchange that echoes through every decision, every gesture, every pause.

Pat Geraghty, president and CEO of GuideWell and Florida Blue, was raised to assume such a role. In the early mornings of his childhood, Geraghty's father would greet him with a saying that subtly, but powerfully, came to shape his understanding of both leadership and life: "Make it a great day." Unlike the more common "Have a great day," this phrase carried a powerful message that would become a cornerstone of Geraghty's leadership philosophy at Prudential Financial, Blue Cross Blue Shield of New Jersey, Blue Cross and Blue Shield of Minnesota, and ultimately as the helm of one of the largest health plans in the United States. The shift from passive to active—the difference between having and making—encapsulated a mindset of ownership, accountability, and proactive engagement.

"When you hear 'Make it a great day' as a young kid, initially, you're rolling your eyes," Geraghty shared with us. "But over time, it sort of sinks in that 'Make it a great day' means you have impact every day, you have the ability to influence what happens to you, or at a minimum, you have an ability to influence how you react to what happens to you, and how you, you internalize the lesson, if you will. So my dad said it all the time. And it's something that I use with my team. And I think it does make a difference here."

When Geraghty first joined GuideWell and Florida Blue, it was clear there were issues—with customers and team members alike. Geraghty didn't just ask for reports on call volumes or issues but made a point of spending time on the front lines, sitting down in the call center and listening in on customer service calls. This was not just a symbolic gesture; it was a deliberate effort to understand the customer experience and the challenges faced by employees in serving them. The impact of this action reverberated throughout the organization, sending a clear message that leadership is not removed from the day-to-day realities of the business.

On the "home front," Geraghty was listening too. He didn't establish committees and wait for bureaucratic recommendations. He asked for input and then put things into action that spoke for themselves. For example, Geraghty eliminated executive parking privileges within twenty-four hours of a suggestion from an employee.

This small but significant change communicated that no one in the organization was above the rest, and it broke down perceived barriers between leadership and staff. These actions were not just about the changes themselves but about what they represented—a commitment to a more egalitarian, inclusive, and responsive organizational culture.

Listening is, indeed, another form of communication. Young Pat Geraghty's household gave him preparation in that arena as well. It was "debate filled," he told us, where dinner conversations were lively discussions about current events and where everyone—children included—were expected to come prepared with facts and reasoned arguments. This environment fostered an appreciation for opinions and a recognition that disagreement, when handled with respect, can lead to better decision-making.

"Our parents encouraged an active, lively, engaged discussion of what was going on in the world," he told us. "And, you know, one of the basic things that come out of that, for me, is I absolutely don't mind being challenged. In fact, I encourage it, and I love when somebody comes well prepared and has thought through their position. And, in fact, at the end of the day, if they have better arguments or a better description of the situation at hand, I'd be foolish not to go with their recommendation. So it creates an environment where I think people understand they contribute. Because it's not a top-down environment. It's a merit-based environment where the best ideas carry the day."

Geraghty also communicates through a sense of calm—a style he attributes in part to inspiration from watching famed basketball coach John Wooden.

"One of my great role models in life was John Wooden, and John Wooden with a rolled-up program in his hand," he said. "But you didn't see him screaming a lot. You know, he was purposeful. He had planned well; he had done all the preparation. And then in the moment, he kept himself grounded. And so it was a role model for me to be thinking about. You have many people that influence your leadership style, and you try to take certain things from them."

Early in his career, Geraghty learned that trying to project an image of perfection was not only unsustainable but also counterproductive. By admitting mistakes and showing vulnerability, he has created a culture where his team feels safe to do the same. This openness fosters a more honest and transparent work environment, where challenges are addressed head-on, and continuous improvement is embraced. Comfort with vulnerability became particularly valuable during times of transformation and restructuring. Geraghty's willingness to acknowledge the difficulties involved in change and to share his own uncertainties has helped to build trust and resilience within his team. By leading with vulnerability, he not only models the behavior he expects from his team but also creates an environment where collaboration and collective problem-solving can thrive.

Geraghty understands that one of the most effective ways to communicate as a leader is through storytelling. Facts and figures are important, but they often fail to inspire. A well-told story, on the other hand, can move people, change mindsets, and drive action. Geraghty uses storytelling to highlight successes, illustrate challenges, and reinforce the values and mission of his organization.

"I believe in the power of storytelling. I think a narrative actually moves the mindset," he said. "And so when you can put in good narrative form what you're about, what you're accomplishing, that is powerful to people. You can pile statistics on folks, and they're just going to, you know, it goes over them. It doesn't necessarily get absorbed, but a good narrative, a great story—that sticks. And so we are very intentional about storytelling. Our communications team is fabulous at leading storytelling and positioning our leaders—not just me but across the leadership team—to be storytellers to make sure we're reinforcing the messages and the learnings and the things that impact our customers. So you got to make it real and personal if you really want to move the way people think about things."

Geraghty's example underscores the many forms that leader comms can, and ideally should, take: His communications take the form of intentionality, debate, calmness, storytelling, and, above all else, action.

This combination delivered a powerful punch for GuideWell under Geraghty's leadership. GuideWell, the holding company for Florida Blue, became the first in the country to transition into a mutual insurance holding company within the health care sector. When they began this process, only two other companies in their state had done something similar, but both were in property and casualty insurance, and it took them eighteen to twenty-four months. GuideWell, however, achieved this transformation in just six months, much faster than anyone had done before. This rapid success challenged the perception that the company was slow and disjointed, demonstrating their ability to work efficiently across divisions.

"People would have told you we're slow, we don't work across divisions, and I made a purposeful demonstration for folks about how fast it was done, how many parts of the organization had to contribute, to get it done," Geraghty said. During this process, GuideWell was at a meeting in Miami with Florida's insurance commissioner for a community event where the public was invited to voice their opinions— and the task ahead was in no way easy.

"Yet, when we went to our membership, 93 percent of our members voted in favor of putting this mutual insurance holding company in place. They're the owners of our organization. So we were breaking down sort of the urban myths about how we moved as a company," Geraghty reflected. "Having those kinds of moments where you can say, we committed to do this, and we committed to do it faster than anyone had done it. We were successful in a very large project. It changed the way people thought about who we were and what we were capable of."

I f you think about leadership as a process, it's really about leveraging influence. And here's the thing—the ability to influence others is closely tied to how well you communicate. If you want to amplify a spark, you have to be able to communicate both the opportunities that spark presents and the reality of it. What does this mean in practice? It's about being clear on three things: Where are we right now? Where do we want to go? And how can we take advantage of this moment?

There's plenty of research to back this up. Multiple studies show just how important leader communication is when it comes to shaping followers' attitudes and intentions. For example, how a leader communicates can boost followers' motivation to complete their tasks, increase their levels of optimism, and even strengthen their sense of organizational support.

David Petraeus in Iraq tried to highlight the ways in which they were making progress: We understand it will be a difficult journey, and here are the things that can help us understand how the actions we are taking will impact our ultimate objective. Whether in sports, business, or politics, it's that ability to communicate effectively that amplifies the ability to influence effectively.

What we're trying to do is help leaders understand how they can amplify the ability to influence others to do things in the best interest of the organization. How do we get them to buy in to whatever it is that needs to be done? Not everyone is going to see the same thing, so it's the leader's job to set the stage and define what's being experienced.

In Petraeus's case, it was the ability to communicate the importance of little wins—not just to tell his people that they were winning but to do so with credibility—because he had told the truth up until then, in good times and bad.

Talking strictly about momentum, the words leaders say are really important. Leaders are what throw fuel—or water—on the spark.

Sometimes, leaders can actually amplify a negative. And in some of these cases, leader communications can stifle productivity and impede momentum. Sometimes, loss aversion is the enemy of opportunity.

Where a tasseographer seeks to elucidate meaning from patterns in the remnants of a person's cup of tea, the business analyst seeks to track and predict markets and performance through data big and small. Tea leaf reading is a form of entertainment, really—not science. But the insights from big data may seem that way, too, to an audience untrained in analytics. Without a way to track, measure, or predict it, momentum is more easily romanticized as a magical force that without preparation or intervention forms an unstoppable snowball effect. But to Guild CEO Rohan Chandran, it's clear that momentum isn't a wave to ride but rather something you must actively create and nurture. And to Chandran, it's the role of the leader to communicate this potential in critical moments.

Chandran would know a thing or two about that—both in corporate life and in being a deep observer of metrics on the sports field. His academic training in economics and computer science has contributed to roles at various major companies, all of which saw transformational growth through Chandran's application of data to strategy.

In the modern corporate landscape, "red teaming" plays a critical role. This strategic approach involves adopting the mindset of an adversary to identify and address vulnerabilities within a company's operations. Companies engage in red teaming to bolster their defenses, ensuring that they are prepared for potential threats. It's a proactive measure that highlights weaknesses before they can be exploited by actual adversaries. This form of security activity is indispensable because it keeps companies on their toes and introduces intentional friction to avoid unforced error. It's akin to having a constant devil's advocate challenging assumptions and exposing blind spots.

But there's a fine line between vigilance and paranoia. Chandran had a front-seat view of perhaps one of the greatest errors of self-protectiveness when serving as an executive at Yahoo. He tells us the story of a specialized team within the organization—the Paranoids—a legendary team within the company, known for its dedication to security and innovation during the early days of the internet. The team got its name due to its intense focus on security, often adopting a mindset of being "paranoid" about potential threats to Yahoo's infrastructure and services. Formed in the mid-1990s, the Paranoids were tasked with protecting Yahoo's rapidly growing web services. As Yahoo expanded, so did the complexity of security challenges, ranging from protecting user data to ensuring the integrity of the company's various platforms. The Paranoids were at the forefront of developing and implementing security measures to safeguard against emerging cyber threats. And they were incredibly good at it.

The Paranoids were known for their rigorous approach to security, using innovative practices to anticipate and mitigate risks. Their culture was one of proactive defense, where thinking like an attacker was key to building robust defenses. This mindset led to the development of many innovative security practices that were ahead of their time. The Paranoids implemented some of the earliest forms of web security protocols, including encryption and authentication methods that became industry standards. They developed comprehensive incident-response strategies that enabled Yahoo to quickly and effectively address security breaches. And the team was also involved in educating Yahoo users about security best practices, helping to raise awareness about online safety.

But while the legacy of the Paranoids at Yahoo is significant in that they laid the groundwork for many of the security practices used in the industry today, it's the innovation that this team may have stifled that left the most lasting mark on the company itself. Instead of seizing opportunities and doubling down on sparks of innovation, the input of the Paranoids often stalled progress out of fear. Chandran reflects on this period, noting how Yahoo dulled its momentum because it was too cautious.

"Yahoo had the potential; it had everything," Chandran told us. "Google plus Meta combined is what Yahoo could and should have been. And we had the talent, the data, and everything to go there."

But despite having the resources to dominate, Yahoo became complacent, satisfied with being in second place to these rising giants. This mindset of settling for less led to missed opportunities and, ultimately, the company's decline from its former glory. Yahoo's approach—its deference to "paranoia" over innovation—is a cautionary tale. At a time when the company could have pushed forward and embraced the rapidly evolving digital landscape, there was too much contentment with maintaining the status quo. Chandran recalls hearing phrases like "Being second in this market overall is not a bad thing," which encapsulates the mindset that leads to stagnation.

Chandran's philosophy on momentum hearkens back to the definition of this phenomenon in physics: Momentum equals mass times velocity. "In business, you may not be able to change the mass or heft of your company instantly, but you can control the speed at which you operate," Chandran explains. "This speed, when directed purposefully, creates momentum."

Chandran illustrates this with a story from his time at Cricinfo. When they saw the potential of the web, they didn't just sit back and watch. They dove in, experimenting and innovating rapidly. They added visuals to what used to be a text-based site and created the first live sports scorecard on the internet. They moved quickly. They created momentum. In stark contrast to how the Paranoids at Yahoo would intentionally, by design, slow things down out of caution for avoiding errors, Cricinfo powered ahead into uncharted territory, risks and all. The decision to do so was a parallel to the role Chandran sees for captains in the game of cricket.

"On the cricket field, you might be waiting all day to take a wicket," he elaborated. "And you've got two batters out there. And they've been going, you know, it's a five-day game, and they've been going for six hours. And you're sort of, what's going to happen here? And then a moment happens because one of the batters is a little tired, and there's an unforced error, if you will; that's not really cricket speak, but it'll work. That moment doesn't create the momentum. What creates momentum is as the captain of that side that's in the field at that point, it's the decisions you make there—a door has been opened, but do you do something about it? And the best leaders in the sports field will react quickly and nimbly to seeing, 'Oh, there was a spark—how do I latch on to it? Can I take advantage of that situation?' In cricket, you'll see the best leaders change strategy in those moments—the field setting changes, your strike bowler comes back on, and they say, 'Can I now create momentum?' And so my point here is that momentum is an intentional thing that you have to participate in creating, not just sit back and hope it happens."

This analogy translates to business leadership. Leaders must be vigilant for opportunities and ready to act swiftly to leverage them. It's about seeing the spark and having the courage and strategy to act upon it—to communicate to one's team that this is the moment, and then together turn it into a blazing fire.

LEADER ACTIONS

There is a saying that "I don't know what I said until you tell me what you heard." The ability to lead well is highly correlated with communications effectiveness. A leader's ability to adroitly provide purpose, direction, and motivation is transmitted through their communications. Effective communication requires transmitting a message from a sender to a receiver using common symbols, with the goal of the receiver accurately understanding the message. Fostering momentum happens in part via written, verbal, and nonverbal mediums. Ensuring your communications are positively driving the desired team behaviors is vitally important.

ACTION 1:
Clearly highlight the importance of significant facts.

A variety of critical communications frameworks details the importance of generating clarity. Momentum is a function of tangible events being linked together. Yet leaders can wrongly believe certain things are patently obvious. Leaders must ensure people understand the significance of what is transpiring.

ACTION 2:
Clearly articulate the way ahead.

The establishment of clear expectations is the first step in creating accountability. For teams to build upon (or reverse) the significance of previous events, leaders must lay out their expectations for what must transpire. The military uses a framework called "leader's intent" as a means for articulating the way ahead. The framework is a concise communications tool that provides three crucial pieces of information: (1) purpose—why the assignment matters; (2) key tasks—what must transpire; and (3) end state—the success criteria. The benefit of the leader's intent framework is that it serves as a vehicle for empowerment. The "why" is provided to place things into context. The "what" is provided to ensure the "must do" smaller elements of the overarching task are understood. Finally, the "what success consists of" statement details how the team will know whether it has won. The intent statement does not articulate the "how" (thus empowering team members to develop plans that will achieve the intent).

ACTION 3:
Consistently ensure two-way communications transpire.

Leaders must cogently convey and receive information. Effective two-way communication can enhance trust, strengthen alignment, and sustain adherence to behavioral expectations. The practice of routinely engaging in two-way communications can foster faster and more effective learning, creating the conditions for better decision-making.

10

Team Climate

arry Ridge made his living reducing friction. He also made his living reducing friction. No, that wasn't a typo or an erroneous repeat. Ridge truly did make his living by literally reducing friction through the product his company made, WD-40, becoming a household go-to, and by reducing friction in the company's organization—between the individuals and hierarchies within it. Perhaps it should be no surprise that Ridge's philosophy of leadership is a match for what his company offers consumers—the promise that when friction is reduced, freedom of movement is possible, and that when movement is possible, momentum is too.

"The opposite of momentum is friction," Ridge told us. "So how do you remove friction that allows you to have momentum? You remove friction by having systems and behaviors in the organization that don't cause churn and that don't stop people from moving on." On one level, Ridge's approach reflects a callback to the Attraction-Selection-Attrition model of recruitment, where through attrition those who are a poor fit for the organization self-select out, making room for individuals who match a team's culture to join and contribute. But Ridge's theory of organizational "freedom" goes well beyond the choice to join or leave the ranks.

"These values that we had were truly the foundation of freedom. People want three things: They want to be able to make their own choice, they want to know they matter, and they want to know they belong. That's it," Ridge shared with our team. "Choice is something that is given to people within a framework because people won't make choices if they feel fear. And so at WD-40, we don't make mistakes; we have learning moments, which are actually catalysts."

Ridge told the story of how WD-40 attempted to introduce a new product but was at first worried about the negative impact to the brand if the product didn't work. To avoid this, they used a different color scheme and omitted the brand's iconic shield—and the product flopped. They learned in that moment the motivating "power of the shield" and readjusted, tinkered with the branding, and tried again.

"It created the opportunity to be able to move on to a new opportunity because people weren't afraid," Ridge said. At WD-40, learning moments became an important part of the culture—a feature, not a bug in a collaborative process that allowed them to take advantage of a spark.

Another such learning moment, early in Ridge's tenure at WD-40, led to perhaps the biggest transformation in his leadership approach. Ridge had just returned to the office from two weeks abroad.

"I remember vividly how it happened," he recounted. "I got back, and I hadn't been in the office for long at all, and someone kind of barreled up to me and said, 'I got to talk to you,' and just dumped on me." This was in the days where email wasn't as prevalent, and Ridge was taken aback.

"If you'd spent as much time finding out or doing something about finding out what you don't know, instead of storing that anger up in your backpack for two weeks, you could've solved the problem," Ridge told his employee, whose response was the spark for major change.

"I didn't have permission."

Ridge began to put in place cultural requirements at WD-40 to avoid repeats of stagnation, confusion, and resentment. "We put in the company permissions and the maniac pledges, which gives people unilateral permission. And we all live it. Live it every day," Ridge explained. Indeed, employees know this pledge, as does anyone who takes a deeper walk through the WD-40 website.

"I am responsible for taking action, asking questions, getting answers, and making decisions," the pledge reads. "I won't wait for someone to tell me. If I need to know, I'm responsible for asking. I have no right to be offended that I didn't 'get this sooner.' If I'm doing something others should know about, I'm responsible for telling them." Ridge explains, "The Maniac Pledge is about the honesty of action and the honesty of communication."

WD-40's culture is one of fearlessness where employees feel safe to take risks, make mistakes, and learn from them without fear of retribution. Ridge understood that for the company to innovate and grow, employees needed to feel empowered and supported. And that, beyond being coworkers, these individuals formed what was really a tribe.

To Ridge, the possibility for momentum is enhanced when a group of people come together as part of something bigger than themselves.

"A group of people going in the same direction are going to have more momentum than a group of individuals running in different directions, right?" Ridge stated more than asked. "When we talk about tribes, we're talking about the behavior of tribes that existed at the beginning of mankind. Now, the thing that was really, really powerful, that was very helpful for me was, the number one responsibility as that of a tribal leader is to be a learner and a teacher. So our whole concept of coaches and teaching and learning was all around, how do we help those we have the privilege to lead step into the better version of themselves? Now, you know, if I was to take you back thousands of years to my homeland, Australia, and we were at, we're actually observing a group of Indigenous Australians, what would the tribal leader be doing? He'd be teaching the younger tribe members to throw a boomerang. Why? Because the boomerang was the tool of survival. And without competency around a boomerang, the tribe would not be able to exist. So this whole tribe thing was, again, it gets back to people wanting to belong. They want to know they're part of something bigger than themselves."

WD-40 tribe members know their company's values, know their company's leaders, and enjoy a sense of belonging and purpose. Like the lubricant they sell to make hinges and other surfaces less sticky, team climate at WD-40 is the formula that reduces friction and drives success.

From nearly the moment of birth, an infant's brain is finely tuned to their mother's voice, face, and scent. You might know this already from observation—but we no longer have to question whether the observed bond between mother and baby is imagined. Through advanced imaging techniques and biometrics, researchers can literally observe and measure what a strong bond between individuals looks like physiologically. Studies utilizing functional magnetic resonance imaging have shown that hearing their mother's voice activates specific regions of an infant's brain more robustly than any other voice. This is true for biological children and adopted children alike.

One study by Abrams et al. (2016) found that when infants hear their mother's voice, there is heightened activity in regions of the brain associated with emotion and reward processing, such as the amygdala and ventral tegmental area. This response was significantly stronger than when the infants were exposed to the voices of unfamiliar women. This suggests that a mother's voice not only soothes and comforts but also plays a critical role in emotional and social development by activating neural circuits linked to bonding and attachment.

The sight of a mother's face is another powerful stimulus for an infant's brain. Research by Bushnell et al. (1989) and subsequent studies have shown that infants as young as a few days old can distinguish their mother's face from those of other women. Using eye-tracking technology and electrophysiological measures, scientists observed that infants spend more time looking at their mother's face and show greater neural activation in the visual cortex. And beyond mere recognition, Haan and Nelson (1997) found that when infants viewed their mother's face, there is increased activity in the fusiform gyrus, a brain region crucial for face recognition. Even the sense of smell plays a significant role in the mother–infant bond. Porter et al. (1992) employed olfactory tests to show that infants, when exposed to breast pads worn by their mothers versus those worn by other women, exhibited distinct behavioral preferences and physiological responses.

Furthermore, studies using near-infrared spectroscopy have found that the brain's olfactory regions light up more intensely when infants are exposed to their mother's scent. This preferential activation suggests that a mother's unique scent not only comforts the infant but also stimulates brain regions associated with recognition and memory, reinforcing the emotional connection. Unsurprisingly, then, the simultaneous exposure to a mother's voice and face results in even more strongly enhanced neural synchrony in the infant's brain.

This type of bonding isn't limited to moms. Research regarding newborn response to fathers and siblings shows similar patterns. And the neurophysiological response to one another is a two-way street. Literally, these new, foundational relationships change how brains function. For example, the transition to fatherhood involves significant changes in brain activity that support bonding and caregiving. A study published in *Social Neuroscience* by Narcis A. Marshall and colleagues (2022) examined brain connectivity in first-time fathers. During the study, expectant fathers underwent functional MRI scans both during their partner's pregnancy and six months after the birth of their child. They found that greater resting-state functional connectivity between regions such as the medial prefrontal cortex and lateral occipital cortex was associated with increased empathy and stronger father–infant bonding. This connectivity was also linked to more supportive and effective parenting behaviors.

Expanding the circle even further, other studies looked at the neurophysiological impacts of sibling contact on babies and found similar results: Infants show increased activation in brain regions associated with social processing when interacting with their older siblings far beyond what is seen when interacting with other children of their siblings' age. Our family is our first team, and our brains get prepped for bonding and social attachment through these early relationships. The power—the potential energy—of cohesion is extraordinary.

Imagine a rowing team, each member perfectly in sync, their strokes harmonizing to propel the boat forward with maximum efficiency. This image epitomizes team cohesion, where the whole becomes greater than the sum of its parts. Any person out of rhythm, in turn, reduces the efficiency of the vessel. Not one member of that team can arrive at a goal before the others. While less obvious to the eye, in the high-stakes world of professional sports, corporate boardrooms, and military units, cohesion is the one crucial element that often determines success. This invisible force binds individuals together, enabling them to function as a unified whole. But what exactly fosters this cohesion, and how does it tangibly affect team performance?

By exploring scientific literature, we can unravel the dynamics behind team cohesion and its pivotal role in achieving collective goals.

At the heart of team cohesion is the simple yet profound phenomenon of interpersonal attraction. When team members genuinely like and respect one another, cohesion naturally follows. Casey-Campbell and Martens (2009) emphasized that positive interpersonal relationships within a team are directly correlated with its cohesiveness. Think of cohesion as the social glue that binds team members, fostering a sense of loyalty and mutual support.

Research underscores that there are a few critical drivers of group cohesion, including mutual respect, a shared sense of purpose, effective communication, and participatory leadership. When team members are united by common goals and a collective vision, their commitment to the team intensifies. Beal et al. (2003) found that goal alignment fosters a sense of unity and direction, making it easier for members to work in sync. This alignment ensures that every member knows their role in the larger scheme and understands how their contributions help achieve the team's objectives.

Effective communication is the lifeline of team cohesion. Open, honest, and frequent communication helps build trust and ensures that everyone is on the same page. Chiocchio and Essiembre (2009) highlighted that a continuous flow of information and feedback creates an environment where cohesion can flourish. In cohesive teams, members feel comfortable voicing their opinions, raising concerns, and brainstorming solutions collectively. The role of leadership in fostering team cohesion cannot be overstated. Leaders who practice participative and supportive leadership styles significantly enhance team cohesion. Grossman et al. (2015) noted that leaders who involve team members in decision-making processes and provide the necessary support cultivate an environment of trust and mutual respect.

This not only strengthens the bonds among team members but also aligns their efforts toward the team's goals.

You may easily be able to conjure images of a sales team participating in a ropes course. But there's a reason outings such as these continue to get scheduled even in the face of the occasional eye roll by skeptics. The academic literature is clear that structured interventions in which team members engage in activities outside of their usual work context play significant roles in enhancing cohesion. Santoro et al. (2015) found that team-building exercises help break down barriers, improve communication, and foster a sense of camaraderie. The physical challenges and shared experiences build trust and cooperation, which translate back to the workplace. Team members who have overcome obstacles together in a recreational setting are more likely to support one another during high-pressure periods.

The impact of cohesion on team performance is profound. Cohesive teams tend to outperform their noncohesive counterparts in various dimensions and exhibit higher levels of productivity and effectiveness. Vanhove and Herian (2015) demonstrated that the strong social bonds and shared goals within cohesive teams drive members to go the "extra mile," ensuring that tasks are accomplished with higher efficiency and quality. This is particularly evident in professional sports teams, where players who have strong off-field relationships often perform better during games, leveraging their trust and understanding to execute complex plays seamlessly.

Members of cohesive teams report higher levels of job satisfaction and motivation. The sense of belonging and mutual support boosts individual morale. Maynard et al. (2015) found that when team members feel connected and valued, their engagement and commitment to the team's objectives increase. In a corporate setting, this translates to lower turnover rates and higher employee retention, as satisfied employees are less likely to seek opportunities elsewhere.

Cohesive teams also show better adaptability in the face of changes and challenges. The robust relationships and effective communication networks within these teams allow for quicker and more effective responses to disruptions. Santoro et al. (2015) observed that cohesive teams are more resilient, capable of navigating uncertainties and maintaining their focus on long-term goals despite setbacks. Cohesive teams are better equipped to handle conflicts constructively. Grossman et al. (2015) noted that the trust and mutual respect in cohesive teams facilitate constructive conflict resolution, ensuring that disagreements do not derail the team's progress but rather serve as opportunities for growth and improvement. In high-pressure environments like law firms, where conflicts can arise frequently, cohesive teams can manage these disputes without losing sight of their objectives, maintaining a high standard of work.

Understanding what makes a team cohesive and how this cohesion affects performance is a complex task. First, it's important to understand that while cohesion is a feeling between people, it is also measurable—sometimes neatly, sometimes subjectively. These measures provide researchers with a way to understand which factors foster cohesion and how cohesion impacts outcomes.

Various methods have been developed and validated to measure the construct of cohesion. One of the most common methods is through questionnaires and self-report measures. These tools are designed to capture individuals' perceptions of team cohesion across different dimensions. The Erlangen Team Cohesion at Work Scale, for example, was developed to measure team cohesion in work settings, particularly in health care. The scale assesses various aspects of team cohesion, including support at work, feedback, sense of community, and perceived social support (*BMC Psychology*, 2023). Similarly, the Perceived Cohesion Scale is a concise measure consisting of six items that assess perceived cohesion, and the Copenhagen Psychosocial

Questionnaire is a broader tool that includes subscales to measure aspects related to team cohesion, such as support at work and sense of community. This questionnaire has shown good reliability and is widely used in various occupational settings to assess psychosocial factors (*BMC Psychology*, 2023).

In addition to self-report questionnaires, observational and behavioral measures provide an external assessor's view of team cohesion. This method can be time intensive but provides valuable insights into the dynamic aspects of team cohesion in which independent researchers observe team interactions to assess behaviors indicative of cohesion, such as collaboration, communication patterns, and mutual support. Sometimes, in this approach, "task-based measures" can be collected when teams are given specific tasks that require collaboration, and their performance is analyzed to infer levels of cohesion. These tasks often include problem-solving activities, simulations, or cooperative games, allowing researchers to observe how well team members work together (*Journal of Business and Psychology* 2012).

The final way to measure cohesion gets more complicated, both in the methodology and in the interpretation of findings. Recent advances have enabled the use of physiological and neurological measures to assess team cohesion, providing insights into the underlying biological mechanisms that drive it and result from it.

Biometrics, such as heart rate variability, skin conductance, and electroencephalography, have been employed to study team dynamics. These measures provide insights into the physiological synchrony among team members, which is a critical component of team cohesion. For instance, a study on sports teams using heart rate variability found that higher cohesion levels were associated with greater physiological synchrony during competitive tasks. Teams with high cohesion demonstrated more synchronized heart rates, indicating a shared physiological response to stress and excitement (Kwon et al., 2024). This synchronization is thought to enhance communication and coordination, leading to better performance. EEG studies in particular have provided valuable insights into the neural synchrony of team members. In one experiment, EEG data revealed that members of cohesive teams had more synchronized brain wave patterns during cooperative tasks compared to noncohesive teams. This neural synchrony is believed to facilitate better communication and coordination, leading to more effective teamwork (*Smithsonian Magazine*, 2020).

Functional MRI studies have furthered our understanding of how team cohesion affects brain activity. One notable study examined brain activity in cohesive versus noncohesive teams during cooperative tasks. Participants from highly cohesive teams showed greater activation in brain regions associated with social cognition, such as the medial prefrontal cortex and temporoparietal junction. These areas are critical for understanding others' intentions and coordinating joint actions (Santoro et al., 2015). Another study using functional MRIs explored how team cohesion influences responses to social exclusion. Members of cohesive teams exhibited less activity in the anterior cingulate cortex, a region linked to the emotional distress of social exclusion. This suggests that cohesive teams provide a buffer against the negative effects of exclusion, enhancing emotional resilience (Maynard et al., 2015).

The complication in interpreting results is that it can be difficult to pull apart the cause of cohesion from the result of it. For instance, in the functional MRI studies that demonstrate how cohesive teams show greater activation in brain regions associated with social cognition and cooperation, this enhanced brain activity is not just a measure of cohesion but also a consequence of it.

Practically speaking, most businesses, sports teams, military units, or other organizations aren't going to have access to functional MRI technology to regularly—if ever—assess how members' brains respond to one another. But the use of regularly fielded questionnaires, and independent observation of collaboration, can give leaders the ability to gauge and benchmark cohesion in their ranks.

There's an important difference between climate and culture. The climate on a team can change with one person, but the culture is more pervasive—it can take years to change a culture. Climate is, perhaps unsurprisingly, more like the weather—reflecting the current state of a work environment based on how cultural norms are being enacted. In a 2017 Medium article, Jason Cummins detailed seven distinctions between climate and culture. Here are some key takeaways and cautions he notes on the difference between climate and culture:

1. Climate is shallow and erratic. Culture is deep and enduring. Climate measures the current organizational temperature. Culture regulates the organizational temperature.

2. Climate is dependent upon present circumstances. Culture withstands present circumstances.

3. A positive climate follows success. A positive culture withstands success.

4. Climate change is easier and can come quickly. Culture change is hard and takes longer than we would desire.

5.   Climate is a team's reaction to present events and circumstances. Culture enables a team to respond to unforeseen events and persevere during difficult circumstances.

6.   Climate leaders are reactionary by nature and prone to choose the quick fix based on short-term results. Culture leaders are intentional by nature and are willing to choose the difficult road that leads to lasting impact.

7.   Positive team climate can lead to a high degree of trust, collaboration, innovation, and engagement, while a negative one can result in conflict, frustration, and poor results.

Leaders must understand what it takes to build a good climate given its immediacy and influence on team members' level of engagement and satisfaction. Key factors like building trust, fostering collaboration, celebrating success, precise communications, and modeling desired behaviors can all help ensure the climate is facilitating a high level of team members' trust and buy-in.

One thing to keep in mind is that recognition plays a big role in this. Recognizing people for their efforts builds trust and celebrates successes at the same time. Research from Quantum Workplace concluded that employees are 2.7 times more likely to be highly engaged if they simply believe they will be recognized. That's a huge difference!

A multiplier of 2.7 is no small thing. It's the difference between traveling at 60 miles per hour or 162. Or the difference between earning 20 percent of a vote or an election-winning 54 percent. It's earning $270 million in a quarter versus $100 million. Or, in a more direct example of engagement, a team member putting in close to 100 percent of one's effort to a project versus significantly less.

Quantum further found that 52.5 percent of their respondents desired more recognition from their first line manager, and 41 percent wanted more recognition from their coworkers and peers. When team members are recognized properly, it goes a long way toward building a positive climate.

UCLA professor Marco Iacoboni didn't set out to study mirror neurons—special brain cells that fire both when an individual performs an action and when they observe someone else performing the same action. Rather, when approached by Giacomo Rizzolatti, the scientist who is credited as discovering mirror neurons, Iacoboni didn't at first agree to collaborate on research of this phenomenon in humans. Iacoboni was, in his own words, "incredulous" at the thought and assumed that, while extraordinarily interesting in concept, mirror neurons were too amazing to be real and must instead be "experimental artifacts."

It was a reasonable level of disbelief for the physician and PhD neuroscientist to have. Indeed, the discovery of mirror neurons had come as a surprise—an incidental finding, if you will—to those who first documented them. Scientists had been observing the monkey brain in the effort to understand what controlled the grasping movement. To their astonishment, the brain regions that "lit up" while a monkey himself grasped an object also fired while the monkey was at rest, watching another grasp an object.

Rizzolatti persisted in his recruitment of Iacoboni to his research team, and he had inspired enough intrigue in Iacoboni that he agreed to visit their lab in Parma, Italy, to learn more. That's when things changed. Iacoboni observed the studies, findings, and anatomies of a discovery that would revolutionize our understanding of human interactions. It would also change the course of Iacoboni's career.

In the late 1990s, Iacoboni and his team at UCLA conducted groundbreaking experiments that provided the first evidence of mirror neurons in humans. These findings, published in his seminal paper "Cortical Mechanisms of Human Imitation" in 1999, opened up new avenues in the study of social cognition and empathy. The implications of this discovery are vast. Mirror neurons suggest that our brains are wired for empathy and understanding others, providing a neural basis for the age-old adage of "walking a mile in someone else's shoes." This neural mirroring process enables humans to understand the actions, intentions, and emotions of others, fundamentally shaping our social interactions and cultural developments.

Iacoboni's work has established that mirror neurons are not just about imitating actions but also about comprehending the intentions behind them ("Grasping the Intentions of Others with One's Own Mirror Neuron System," 2005), and how these neurons affect everything from learning and language development to empathy and social bonding, making a compelling case for the centrality of these neurons in human experience ("Mirroring People: The New Science of How We Connect with Others," 2008).

We were thrilled that Iacoboni agreed to sit for an interview with us early in our project. We had learned of Iacoboni through colleagues, who described him as both intellectually rigorous and deeply empathetic, a combination that mirrors his approach to research and the very topic of its study. More than anything, we wanted to hear Iacoboni's unfiltered thoughts on the question of whether there could be a relationship between mirror neurons and group momentum.

"Imitation is a way of building trust and empathy from the bottom up in teams," Iacoboni shared with us. "It's fairly easy to do in different practices. You can practice individually, but you can also build the practice in a way which results in a lot of imitation between teammates, which can create more sense of belonging."

Iacoboni sprinkles philosophy into his answers—quoting Roman emperor Marcus Aurelius and drawing attention to a core tenet of the stoic mindset: "What really matters is not what happens to you, but how you react," Iacoboni told us, suggesting that empathy between team members can even help insulate individuals from negative spirals following mistakes. And that's not the only way mirror neurons may influence the group experience of (or likelihood for) momentum. Mirror neurons relate to various other aspects of organizational momentum.

- *Role modeling by leaders:* Leaders in organizations often set examples through their behavior, work ethic, and attitudes. When leaders demonstrate high energy, commitment, and strategic vision, mirror neurons in employees can lead them to imitate these behaviors, creating a ripple effect of positive actions and attitudes across the organization.

- *Emotional contagion:* Mirror neurons play a crucial role in emotional contagion, where the emotions of one person can be mirrored and shared by others. In organizations, when key individuals or groups exhibit positive emotions, such as enthusiasm and optimism, these feelings can spread throughout the organization, enhancing morale and collective motivation.

- *Shared goals and vision:* Mirror neurons help individuals understand and internalize the intentions and goals of others. In an organizational context, when leaders and managers effectively communicate a clear and compelling vision, employees are more likely to align their own goals with this vision, creating unified momentum toward organizational objectives.

- *Coordination of efforts:* Effective collaboration and teamwork often rely on the ability to anticipate and respond to the actions of others. Mirror neurons enhance this ability, allowing team members to synchronize their efforts and work more efficiently toward common goals. This coordinated effort can drive organizational momentum, as teams move in harmony toward achieving targets.

Henry Ford once said, "Coming together is a beginning, staying together is progress, and working together is success." Team climate can influence all three things. Leaders must ensure a positive climate exists in addition to an effective culture. Here are three actions leaders can take in pursuit of that obligation.

ACTION 1:
Enhance psychological safety.

In his book *The 4 Stages of Psychological Safety*, Timothy R. Clark describes four key elements or "stages" required for a psychologically safe environment:

1. **Inclusion:** People feel accepted in the workplace.

2. **Learning:** Team members feel safe asking questions, making mistakes, and giving feedback.

3. **Contributing:** Team members feel confident and comfortable making their own contributions to the team.

4. **Challenging:** All team members feel they can question or even criticize processes and protocols when they see something could be improved.

ACTION 2:
Routinely recognize teams and team members who are meeting expectations.

Leaders must reward accomplishments to motivate team members to continue working hard in service of meeting or exceeding standards. A 2022 *Harvard Business Review* article by Jack Zenger and Joseph Folkman references a study regarding employee engagement and recognition. The study examined tens of thousands of 360-degree assessments conducted by the firm Zenger Folkman. Leaders rated in the top 10 percent for providing recognition achieved an average employee engagement percentile of 69.8. Conversely, leaders rated in the bottom 10 percent achieved an average employee engagement percentile of 27.4.

ACTION 3:
Routinely ask for feedback.

For leaders to understand how their actions are being received, they must receive objective feedback. The book *Thanks for the Feedback: The Science and Art of Receiving Feedback* by Sheila Heen and Douglas Stone details a simple practice that can enhance the likelihood of receiving feedback and its quality. They encourage people not to ask for broad, open-ended feedback. Instead, their research has concluded that asking people for "one thing" is more effective. For example, such a question could be structured as follows: "What's one thing you would encourage us to keep doing?" Receiving effective feedback can aid leaders in serving as more effective agents for their teams.

11

Belief and Mindset

T he University of Oregon's gymnasium was a cauldron of anticipation that night. The Ducks women's basketball team, ranked second in the nation, was expected to dominate against UCLA's then unranked team. But somewhere amid the frenzy of the crowd and the intensity of the game, UCLA's head coach, Cori Close, observed something peculiar: Her team, facing a daunting 21-point deficit, displayed an unusual calm. Their body language, far from defeated, was almost serene. It looked like they knew something that the roaring sea of Oregon fans did not.

Close watched from the sidelines, her pulse quickening with the mounting pressure. Yet her players exuded a quiet confidence. They moved with a steadiness that belied the score. Every gesture, every movement suggested not just hope but an unwavering expectation. It wasn't bravado; it was belief. As the minutes ticked away, the Bruins chipped away at Oregon's lead, point by point, possession by possession.

"I saw it in their eyes," Close told us just a year later. "They had this expectant look, like they knew our moment was coming." This wasn't just a coach's wishful thinking. The players' demeanor was infectious, a silent communication of certainty that transcended words. Even as Close's own nerves frayed, her team remained composed, their belief unshaken, and this mindset was shared and reinforced through their body language. By halftime, the impossible seemed suddenly plausible. UCLA had cut the lead to eight, a significant shift from the twenty-one-point chasm that had once yawned between the teams. The momentum was tangible, a shift in the air that Close could almost touch. The Bruins had scored the last six points of the half, and with each basket, the noise in the building transformed. The raucous home crowd grew quieter, the Ducks' body language more strained.

In the locker room, Close saw that the team's calm was not just a front. They huddled together, their conversations reflecting a shared belief that their time had come. "Our language never changed," Close noted. "Even when we were down, they spoke like we were going to win. It was remarkable." This shared mindset was evident in their actions and the way they carried themselves; it was a collective belief. The second half was a testament to this mindset. UCLA played not just to catch up but to win. The momentum had shifted, and Close saw how it affected everything—the noise level, the opposing team's composure, and the very atmosphere of the game. The Ducks, once so dominant, now seemed tentative, their confidence shaken by the unrelenting advance of their opponents.

With about a minute and a half remaining in the game, Close knew her players were exhausted from the energy it took to sustain the comeback. She wanted to call a time-out and call in relief, but her assistant coach knew otherwise. "He was wiser than I was," Close considered. "He was like, you know, we have to ride momentum here. And he was right." As the final buzzer sounded, it was UCLA that stood victorious. They had handed Oregon their only home loss of the season, a feat that seemed impossible just an hour before. Close reflected on that night as a defining moment, not just for the win but for the way it happened. "We stayed expectant," she said, marveling at the power of belief.

This game was not just a comeback; it was a lesson in the power of mindset. Close would carry this lesson with her, recognizing that the power of belief and body language of calm expectancy could indeed shape outcomes in ways she hadn't fully appreciated before. The shared mindset among her players, communicated in how they moved, stood, and saw one another, had turned the tide in their favor and underscored the profound impact of collective belief.

Beliefs are what individuals and organizations hold to be true, such as the conviction or acceptance that something exists. Beliefs may be based on evidence, faith, personal experience, or cultural and societal influences. And beliefs can be about tangible aspects of the world, such as believing in the existence of gravity, or intangible ones, such as believing in fairness or justice. But, in general, beliefs tend to be fairly specific in scope. For example, Victor Vroom, a longtime professor at Yale's School of Management, developed a motivational framework (expectancy theory) that explains how people choose to act based on their expectations of the outcomes. The theory examines three relationships regarding an individual's belief in the likelihood of something transpiring. The first relationship was called "expectancy." It essentially asks the question "If I try it, can I do it?" The second relationship was called "instrumentality." This relationship poses the question "If I do it, will I get the reward?" Finally, the third relationship was called "valence." It asks the question "If I get the reward, will I value it?" If someone possesses a weak belief in any one of the relationships, motivation is lowered.

Mindsets, on the other hand, are a way of thinking or relating to these shared beliefs and become a set of attitudes or ideas that influence behaviors and outlooks. Mindsets are broader and encompass various beliefs that collectively determine one's approach to life, challenges, and opportunities. While beliefs form the foundation of mindsets—in that what someone believes about themselves, others, and the world shapes their mindset—the latter concept has a far more overarching influence on behavior.

It's no surprise, then, that beliefs are more easily changed than mindsets. One may be persuaded by new facts and change beliefs or even assumptions about a person, event, or environment around them, but changing mindsets requires something to influence several interconnected beliefs. And some types of individual or group mindsets are structured in ways that influence how easily they can be changed.

Thanks to research advanced and popularized by Stanford University psychologist Carol Dweck, mindsets can be broadly categorized into two types: growth and fixed. Those with a growth mindset tend to believe that abilities and intelligence can be developed and improved over time through effort, learning, and perseverance. Individuals with a growth mindset see challenges as opportunities to grow, view effort as the path to mastery, and believe that failures are valuable learning experiences.

To the contrary, those with a fixed mindset tend to believe that abilities and intelligence are static traits that cannot be significantly developed. Individuals and group cultures with a fixed mindset tend to avoid challenges, give up easily when faced with obstacles, and see effort as fruitless if natural talent is not present.

Where those with a growth mindset welcome feedback, those with a fixed mindset are more likely to become defensive or dismissive of input. Growth mindsets embrace challenge, tend to persist and adapt to changing plans, and see effort as related to success. All of these characteristics are important to the discussion of group culture and group momentum, but perhaps more than anything is the capacity for those with a growth mindset to *change their mindset.*

At the very least, belief and mindset are complementary concepts, but when it comes to manipulating momentum, our model suggests that both are essential. Members of a team can believe that momentum is real. But if they don't share a common mindset or ethos of how to approach momentum, opportunities will quickly be lost.

B elief and mindset—the "I believe" of momentum—can't be overstated. When things aren't working quite right, some have a sense of panic. But if members of a team believe that they've done all of the things we've been talking about so far—they've prepared, they've brought the right people in, the right culture is in place, a spark has happened, the leader is amplifying it, they're collectively clicking with a great team climate—then, yes, they will have a sense that "we can make this happen."

A lbert Bandura was born on December 4, 1925, in the small town of Mundare, Alberta, Canada. Growing up in a rural community, Bandura developed a strong sense of curiosity and self-reliance, and as the youngest of six children, Bandura spent a lot of time watching and learning from his older siblings. These traits and experiences ultimately shaped what Bandura would come to study in his renowned career in psychology. After completing his undergraduate studies at the University of British Columbia, Bandura pursued his PhD in clinical psychology at the University of Iowa, where he was influenced by the behaviorist tradition but also began to explore new ways of understanding human thought and action.

Bandura's groundbreaking research in the 1960s introduced the world to the concept of social learning theory, which posits that people learn behaviors through observation, imitation, and modeling.

One of his most famous studies, the Bobo doll experiment, vividly illustrated this theory. In this study, children watched an adult model act aggressively toward a Bobo doll, a large inflatable toy. The adult hit, kicked, and verbally assaulted the doll. When the children were later given the opportunity to play with the Bobo doll, they imitated the aggressive actions they had observed, often replicating the exact behaviors and even inventing new ways to attack the doll. This experiment demonstrated that children could learn and replicate aggressive behaviors simply by observing others, without any direct reinforcement.

Building on his work in social learning, Bandura developed the concept of self-efficacy, which he detailed extensively in his later research. Self-efficacy refers to an individual's belief in their ability to execute behaviors necessary to attain their goals. One significant finding from Bandura's research on self-efficacy was its impact on motivation and resilience. For example, Bandura discovered that individuals with high self-efficacy are more likely to set challenging goals, persist through difficulties, and recover quickly from setbacks. They approach tasks with a sense of confidence and are more resilient in the face of adversity compared to those with low self-efficacy, who may doubt their abilities and give up more easily.

The four main sources of information that inform how people conceive of their self-efficacy are as follows: (1) mastery experiences—achieving success at a new task can help build self-belief; (2) vicarious experiences—adopting the experiences of others as our own can help estimate the likelihood of success or failure in similar situations; (3) social persuasion—dialoguing with others can influence self-perception; and (4) physiological and affective states—how we interpret our emotional and physical reactions can affect self-efficacy.

In the 1990s, sociologists Robert Sampson, Stephen Raudenbush, and Felton Earls built upon Bandura's research in a landmark study that underscored the importance of collective efficacy in community settings. Their design, which focused on Chicago neighborhoods, found that areas with high collective efficacy—characterized by mutual trust among neighbors and a shared willingness to intervene for the common good—experienced significantly lower rates of vio lence and crime. This finding highlighted how the collective belief in a community's ability to maintain social order and achieve positive outcomes can dramatically impact real-world conditions.

The power of collective efficacy also touched the 1980 US Olympic hockey team, in a game famously known as the "Miracle on Ice." This group of amateur and collegiate players faced the seemingly insurmountable challenge of competing against the Soviet Union's seasoned and dominant team. Though the Soviets called their team "amateur," their players were all part of the nation's military and played together constantly. They had won the four previous gold medals. Under the leadership of Coach Herb Brooks, the US team cultivated a strong sense of collective efficacy. Brooks instilled confidence in his players through rigorous training, clear goals, and unwavering belief in their potential. The result was one of the most memorable upsets in sports history, as the US team defeated the Soviets and went on to win the gold medal. This victory was not merely the triumph of individual talent but a testament to the power of collective efficacy.

Beyond structured social experiments and sports, Bandura's research also set the stage for a deeper understanding of how self- and group efficacy influences outcomes in business and how leaders can foster collective efficacy within their organizations. We were fortunate for the chance to interview one great mind whose work on leadership, team dynamics, and group efficacy has brought academic research out of the ivory tower and into practical application for teams of all kinds.

John Hollenbeck runs the Team Lab at Michigan State University's Eli Broad College of Business. His research and citations to his work flood academic journals and popular magazines alike, providing scientists across various academic fields with tested theories to explore and providing workplaces with increasingly tactical advice, such as the optimal number of participants on video conference calls. The Department of Defense and the National Science Foundation have both called upon Hollenbeck to explore issues of importance to their respective teams, and when we called upon him to learn more about what might foster team momentum, he was generous in giving us some of his time and insights too.

Hollenbeck's approach to studying the science of group dynamics necessitates a fair amount of natural skepticism about what's real versus perceived, and that orientation was evident in Hollenbeck's initial reaction to our questions of him on momentum. In many instances, Hollenbeck told us, he thinks that momentum is an "epiphenomenon"—an experience that's more perceived than real, born through people seeing patterns and assuming causal relationships between things where none may truly exist.

"The human brain has a natural tendency to detect associations," Hollenbeck explained. One illustration is the "hot hand fallacy" where a series of successes is interpreted by observers—or the performer herself—as a streak of momentum but may or may not be exceptional beyond chance. For example, an NBA player hitting multiple shots in a row is often seen as "hot," but as far as statistical probability, the streak may be indistinguishable from chance.

But despite this uncertainty, to Hollenbeck, the question of "momentum or not?" is less meaningful than the question of how individual and team performance influences self-efficacy, or the belief in one's ability, and how these beliefs, mindsets, and emotions spread through a group, influencing future performance and the potential for sustained momentum. In other words, even if the science is unclear on which events are true momentum and which can be predicted by chance, it may be a distinction without a difference when it comes to how team members perceive these experiences and act upon them. On a practical level, Hollenbeck's scholarship tells us that a team's belief that momentum is on their side can boost collective confidence and effort, even if the actual phenomenon is statistically insignificant.

W hat do most people think of momentum, and do these perceptions differ between people who have more or less experience with team dynamics? In order to learn more about how people perceive momentum, and about how different types of people experience this phenomenon or attempt to manipulate its course in their professional lives, we fielded a series of comprehensive, scientific surveys on this and more, with fifteen hundred American adults responding. The results demonstrate extraordinary consensus on a number of things.

For starters, greater than nine in ten (91 percent) say they believe momentum is "real" when it comes to group experiences such as in sports, business, politics, or the military. But critically, this view is held by greater portions of those who themselves are a member of some type of organized group (93 percent) compared with those who aren't (74 percent). In particular, momentum is perceived as real by greater portions of those who are members of military (98 percent), sports (97 percent), political (96 percent), business (94 percent), and religious (94 percent) groups. This is a huge finding, because across other types of demographic groups, we found few to no differences. The belief in momentum's realness is held by statistically equal portions of men and women; White and non-White individuals; introverts and extroverts; Democrats and Republicans; those who are married, divorced, or single; and those of all sexual orientations. In other words, the real differentiator when it comes to believing in momentum is having been part of a team. And the more teams a person reports they've been a part of, the greater the likelihood that they believe in the realness of momentum.

The perceived experience of momentum in one's own life is equally widespread at least in the aggregate. More than nine in ten (92 percent) say they've experienced (or, importantly, witnessed) what they believe to be momentum in at least one area of life, whether in relationships (62 percent), sports (55 percent), fitness or wellness (47 percent), business or finance (46 percent), politics (39 percent), religion or spirituality (36 percent), or military efforts (30 percent). The belief that one has experienced or witnessed momentum in at least one area of life largely cuts across demographic groups and personal identities, with about equal response between members of all age groups; Democrats and Republicans; those who are married, single, and divorced; gay and straight; White and non-White.

That said, the perceived experience of individual momentum is expressed by greater portions of a few types of people. Specifically, personal experiences with momentum are reported by greater portions of men (95 percent) compared with women (90 percent), extroverts (98 percent) compared with introverts (92 percent), those in households with incomes of $50,000 per year or more (95 percent) compared with those living in households earning less than $50,000 per year (89 percent), and those who are a member of some kind of team (96 percent) compared with those who are not (69 percent). This latter feature—team or group membership—once again demonstrates the most profound difference in the experience of momentum. And a few types of group members report the highest rates of perceived momentum: Those who have served in the military (99 percent), on sports teams (98 percent), in political organizations (98 percent), in business (97 percent), and in religious organizations (96 percent) all express greater belief that momentum has touched their lives compared with those who haven't participated in these types of groups.

Further, a full nine in ten (90 percent) believe that certain conditions can help create momentum or make it more possible for a team or organization to experience, while 10 percent believe that momentum is mostly random and can't be influenced. The perception that momentum can be fostered through certain conditions, once again, is held by greater portions of those who themselves are members of groups (92 percent) compared with those who aren't (83 percent). This question is our closest measure of self-efficacy, which both Bandura and Hollenbeck described as the belief in one's ability to influence personal or group outcomes.

Group membership is pretty common, at least as we've defined it: Seven in ten of those we surveyed say they belong to at least one type of organization that meets regularly and pursues shared goals. Yet even among these individuals who belong to groups and believe that momentum can be influenced by certain conditions, only one in four (25 percent) says they regularly discuss momentum with other group members, and that same portion—26 percent—says they never do so. Looking more closely at members of certain groups, the lack of regular discussion on momentum becomes even more striking. For example, among members of military teams, 98 percent believe momentum is real, 99 percent believe they've experienced it in their own lives, and 95 percent believe that certain conditions can help create momentum for a group—yet just 35 percent say they regularly discuss momentum with their unit. Similarly, among those in business groups, 94 percent believe momentum is real, 97 percent believe they've experienced it in their own lives, and 93 percent believe that certain conditions can help create momentum for a group—yet just 30 percent say they regularly discuss momentum with their unit. This same pattern holds for athletes and political professionals as well: There's widespread belief in the realness of momentum, firsthand experience with it, and the belief that groups can create conditions that make momentum more likely—yet very few are talking about how they can actually do so.

Perhaps this suggests a lack of understanding of where to start that conversation. But overall, these findings illustrate widespread belief in momentum, particularly among people who are engaged with teams of some kind and reflect a collective mindset that is high in self-efficacy—a starting point that is ripe for such conversations to take hold.

Our findings get even a little more telling when looking at specifically what things people believe can increase the likelihood of a team experiencing momentum. We asked respondents to tell us which factors—which components of our model—they believe have the greatest influence on a team's likelihood of experiencing momentum. The two factors that compete with each other for the top spot are group leadership and group chemistry. Rated independently, equal shares—86 percent—feel that group leadership and team climate, respectively, have strong influences over an organization's likelihood of momentum. Team climate is seen as particularly important for under the age of thirty, while leadership is seen as relatively more important by those ages thirty and older.

And perhaps most interesting from a metapsychological perspective, the conviction that beliefs and mindset matter significantly to the experience of group momentum is extraordinarily high. Greater than eight in ten (82 percent) say that beliefs and mindset strongly influence group momentum—tied with the influence of positive or negative feedback (82 percent). This exceeds other factors of the model, including group culture (80 percent), the ability to recognize an external spark for momentum (75 percent), preparation for momentum (69 percent), and how group members are recruited (66 percent). But in other terms, belief and mindset are seen as having little to no influence by just 18 percent.

Maybe, in some respects, when it comes to momentum, to believe it is to see it.

It may not require every member of a team to believe that momentum is real or that momentum is happening at the outset of a spark in order for its potential to take hold. But having *some* members of an organization believe it and share this perception does seem to matter. Beliefs, like tangible molecules, can spread between people—as do emotions. Emotional contagion, the phenomenon where emotions spread from person to person, has been extensively studied in various social contexts. Research defines emotional contagion as the automatic and unconscious transmission of emotions between individuals, often occurring through nonverbal cues like facial expressions, body language, and tone of voice. This process can have significant implications for individual behavior and group dynamics.

The implications of emotional contagion for group performance are profound and can involve both positive and negative emotions. Positive emotional contagion can enhance group cohesion and can lead to higher levels of cooperation, better problem-solving, and increased motivation. This is particularly relevant in organizational settings, where the mood and emotional tone set by leaders can trickle down to affect the entire team's performance (Hennig-Thurau et al., 2006). For example, in a study on workplace dynamics, it was found that positive emotions expressed by leaders can significantly boost the morale and performance of their teams (Hennig-Thurau et al., 2006). On the other hand, negative emotional contagion can lead to increased stress and reduced productivity. Left unchecked, negative emotional contagion can result in conflicts, decreased motivation, and lower overall productivity. Studies in clinical settings have shown that the spread of negative emotions can exacerbate mental health issues, such as depression and anxiety, among patients and caregivers (*Journal of Business and Psychology* 2011).

Emotional contagion is facilitated by several mechanisms. Key among them is a process called mimicry, where individuals unconsciously imitate the emotional expressions of others, leading to a shared emotional experience. Here's the interesting part: This process is largely automatic and can occur without conscious awareness. Studies have shown that when people observe others expressing emotions, they tend to mimic these expressions, which can then trigger similar emotional states in themselves (Hatfield, Cacioppo & Rapson 1994).

Several factors can influence the extent to which emotional contagion occurs within groups. The intensity and frequency of emotional expressions play a crucial role. More intense and frequent emotional displays are more likely to be contagious. Social context and relationships between individuals also matter. In close-knit groups or teams, emotional contagion is more pronounced due to stronger interpersonal bonds and greater empathy among members (*PNAS* 2014). Interestingly, the medium of communication can also impact emotional contagion. While traditionally studied in face-to-face interactions, research has shown that emotional contagion can occur in online environments. For instance, large-scale studies on social media platforms like Facebook have demonstrated that emotions expressed in status updates can influence the emotions of others, even without direct physical interaction (*PNAS* 2014).

The susceptibility to emotional contagion also varies among individuals. It should come as no surprise that some people are more naturally susceptive than others, and research has illuminated that certain personality traits can make individuals more prone to emotional contagion. For instance, people with high levels of empathy or those who are more attuned to social cues are often more susceptible. On the flip side, individuals with traits such as psychopathy, characterized by low empathy, are less likely to experience emotional contagion (*PLOS ONE* 2021).

About two hours and forty-five minutes south of Marco Iacoboni, neuroscientist Jaime Pineda sits in his office at the University of California, San Diego. Like Iacoboni, Pineda's research has contributed significantly to the understanding of mirror neurons, consciousness, and empathy, and the two scientists have even coauthored some studies. We wanted to learn more about emotional contagion, in particular, and about how shared emotional experiences can affect team performance. Pineda was uncertain that he'd have much to offer us.

"I'm not sure how much I can share with you, or whatever could be useful, but I'm willing to do it," Pineda said as we hit RECORD and began the interview. His humility was admirable, but his prediction was way off—in a short twenty-three minutes, Pineda gave quite a lot to think about and, beyond that, take action on.

If you recall, mirror neurons are activated both when an individual performs an action and when they observe someone else performing the same action. This mirroring mechanism is fundamental to empathy and social bonding because it allows individuals to resonate with the emotions of others. According to Pineda, mirror neurons are highly sensitive to social and environmental cues. We asked whether mirror neurons differentiate between observing a friend or a colleague achieve success versus watching someone on another team or someone on TV, and Pineda believes this is so.

"The evidence suggests that mirror neurons do differ based on familiarity," he said. "If you're familiar with someone, you tend to mirror them more than somebody who is unfamiliar. In general, the literature shows that anyone that's like you, similar to you, we tend to mirror them more than somebody who is unlike us."

The activity of mirror neurons can be measured through a process known as mu suppression. Mu rhythms are brain waves that diminish in amplitude when an individual engages in or observes movement, providing a biomarker for mirror neuron activity. Research has shown that mu suppression is linked to the activation of mirror neurons, thus serving as a reliable index for studying emotional contagion. These brain rhythms can become synchronized when individuals engage in common tasks, indicating effective communication and collaboration.

Pineda explains that synchronized brain activity is crucial for cognitive functions such as working memory and attention, and in the context of team dynamics, synchronized brain activity among team members can enhance cooperation and collective performance. For instance, studies have shown that teams with higher levels of neural synchrony perform better in tasks that require close coordination and communication.

"When brains become synchronized, sort of the analog of that, that these two brains are somehow communicating in some way that we really don't know yet," Pineda elaborated. "And our studies show that things like working memory are affected by how synchronized certain parts of the brain are, like the frontal cortex needs to be synchronized in order for there to be better working memory."

It's also clear that emotional contagion can lead to the creation of psychological momentum within a team. This momentum is characterized by a sense of collective efficacy and motivation, which propels the team toward achieving their goals. Pineda highlighted for us that fostering a positive emotional environment is essential for triggering this momentum. Leaders and team members can facilitate positive emotional contagion by displaying enthusiasm, support, and empathy, which in turn can inspire and energize the entire group. Moreover, he shared that the desire for social connection plays a significant role in emotional contagion. When individuals have a strong desire to connect and empathize with others, they are more likely to engage in mirroring behaviors. This social bonding can amplify the positive emotions within the group, leading to a self-reinforcing cycle of motivation and performance.

These findings suggest several practical approaches for leveraging emotional contagion to build momentum in teams. These include:

- Setting positive expectations: Establishing a positive vision and clear goals can motivate team members and foster a sense of shared purpose.

- Promoting curiosity and empathy: Encouraging team members to be curious and empathetic toward one another can strengthen social bonds and enhance emotional contagion.

- Utilizing neurofeedback: Implementing neurofeedback techniques can help individuals synchronize their brain activity, leading to improved cognitive function and emotional regulation.

- Encouraging meditation: Activities such as meditation can induce synchronized brain states, promoting relaxation and reducing stress within the team.

Resilience, optimism, motivation, and other aspects of team life are influenced by belief and mindset. In psychology, a belief is a mental state or disposition that is often associated with a particular response, whereas motivation is the force that drives people to act and pursue specific goals or objectives. We can characterize the difference between belief and motivation with two questions. "Do you think we have what it will take to succeed?" and "Are you inclined to do what it will take to succeed?" Leaders must harness the power of belief in their teams and create a mindset that maintains people's motivation to do the work.

ACTION 1:
Frame things positively.

Positive framing is a technique that involves presenting information in a way that influences how it's perceived and received. There are numerous ways to use this practice. Here are three examples: (1) focus on gains—emphasize the benefits and opportunities of your message, rather than the costs and risks. You can also provide context and comparisons that put your message in a favorable light; (2) use positive words—use words and phrases that convey optimism, confidence, and enthusiasm; and (3) give examples—provide specific examples that illustrate the positive impact of your message.

ACTION 2:
Ensure your team has high expectancy.

Psychologist Victor Vroom's expectancy theory of motivation originally examined motivational factors for individuals. But later research concluded the construct could also be applied to teams. The theory asserts behavior is motivated by anticipated results or consequences, and the intensity of the subject's work is driven by the perception that their effort will lead to a desired outcome. The three major components of the theory examine the relationships between task behavior, performance outcome, and reward valence. Most importantly, the relationship between task behavior and performance outcome is called "expectancy." In many instances, the relationship is characterized by the question "Do I believe that if I try it I can do it?" When the expectancy relationship is weak, motivation is lowered. Ensuring that your team has strong expectancy can be achieved through a variety of means (for example, provide training and resources, create a supportive environment, set clear expectations, provide regular feedback).

ACTION 3:
Encourage a growth mindset.

This concept was developed by Stanford psychologist Carol Dweck. It involves seeing challenges and feedback as opportunities for growth and improvement. You can model this by embracing challenges, seeking feedback, and learning from mistakes. When Satya Nadella took over Microsoft in 2014, he mandated that his senior leadership team read Dweck's book *Mindset*. Ultimately, he held everyone at the company accountable for moving from a "know it all mindset" to a "learn it all mindset." The resulting shift in mindset and culture played a huge role in Microsoft's ability to successfully pivot into becoming a services company (and in doing so unlocking more than $2.75 trillion in market capitalization over the course of a decade).

12

Outcomes
and Feedback

Everyone knows that to be a fighter pilot in the US military you need to have good eyesight. That's just the start. You need a bachelor's degree, preferably in an area such as engineering or math, and exceptional cardiovascular health to handle extreme g-forces. You need to excel on a series of tests in reasoning, problem-solving, mechanical systems, reading, special apperception, and aviation and naval principles. You need to rank strongly in a battery of personality assessments regarding stress management, leadership, and decision-making. And all of that's before fight training begins.

Pilots are responsible not only for their life and limb, and those of the troops or civilians they're deployed to protect, but also for about $100 million in the aircraft they're controlling. The responsibility is high, the stakes are high, and recruitment into these positions is fine-tuned to ensure the best possible chances of success for the team.

For a select few elite fighter pilots, joining the Blue Angels flight demonstration squadron is an even higher honor and responsibility. Acceptance into the Blue Angels program is one of the most prestigious assignments a Navy or Marine Corps pilot can receive. It's extremely competitive, and only the most skilled and experienced pilots are chosen. These are the pilots with extensive flight hours, often in combat situations, who have exhibited exceptional skills flying in close formations with complex aerobatic routines. They have to be carrier qualified, meaning they have experience landing on aircraft carriers, and they're almost always at the rank of lieutenant commander or major. These pilots are expected to serve as ambassadors for the Navy and Marine Corps, showcasing the professionalism and capabilities of these services to the public. In this capacity, Blue Angels don't just fly but also are expected to interact with communities, inspiring young people and representing the US armed forces at events across the country.

Recruitment for the Blue Angels includes an element not often seen in military—or, really, most—contexts: peer selection. In this, current members of the Blue Angels play a significant role in selecting new team members.

The Blue Angels operate in an environment where trust and cohesion are paramount. The peer selection process is designed to ensure that every member can rely on one another implicitly, which is critical for the safety and success of their high-risk performances. Blue Angels candidates are closely observed during training sessions. Current team members assess how the candidate performs under pressure, their adaptability to the team's specific flying style, and their ability to learn and execute the precise maneuvers required. The team looks not only at the applicant's flying skills but also at their personality, how well they work with others, and whether they would fit into the team's close-knit culture. This ensures that the pilots chosen are not only capable but also fit well with the team's culture and dynamics.

Remarkably, the final decision on who is selected is made through a voting process by the current members of the Blue Angels team. Each pilot on the team has a say, and unanimity is often required for a candidate to be accepted. By comparison, while acceptance into other elite military teams such as the Green Berets or Navy SEALs includes observation and assessment of how well candidates perform in coordination with their peers, the final decisions on who gets in are made by instructors.

This isn't the only aspect of the Blue Angels process that is unusually flat or egalitarian, rather than hierarchical, in how they operate. Their feedback process is too. It's a rank-free, brutally candid process that requires prospective Blue Angels pilots to exhibit not only the aforementioned exceptional eyesight, stamina, focus, knowledge, and teamwork. They have to have exceptionally thick skin too.

W hen we first sat down to speak with Commander Alexander P. Armatas, he was the commanding officer of the Blue Angels for the 2023 and 2024 air show seasons. Originally from Skaneateles, New York, Armatas has had a distinguished career in naval aviation. He graduated from the United States Naval Academy in 2002 with a degree in aerospace engineering and earned his wings in 2005. Before taking command of the Blue Angels, Armatas served as the commanding officer of Strike Fighter Squadron 105 (VFA-105), also known as the "Gunslingers." His leadership experience includes multiple deployments aboard aircraft carriers in support of various operations, such as Operation Freedom's Sentinel. Armatas had accumulated more than four thousand flight hours and more than nine hundred carrier-arrested landings when we spoke. And beyond a tally of these flight hours—and of particular interest to our discussion of team dynamics and momentum—Armatas had led and participated in countless hours of debriefs with his teams, the feedback sessions that follow each show. These debriefs often last longer than the event being briefed. While a Blue Angels show may last forty-five minutes, the debriefs last anywhere from one hour to seven. And while the cheering crowds on the grounds offer nearly unanimous positive feedback for the great feats they just observed, the Blue Angels debrief sessions focus almost exclusively on what went wrong.

"That's how we operate," Armatas told us. "We don't have time to pat each other on the back and talk about all the good things. And we did enough things wrong that that'll take up plenty of time on its own. So that's where we focus; we focus on improving on the stuff we did wrong and accepting that the stuff we did right we're going to do right again, which is important as well."

Armatas knows that these things change too—that something that went well on one show may go poorly in the next. There's so little room for error that feedback must be equally clear. After all, these pilots fly within eighteen inches wingtip-to-wingtip of one another at speeds up to seven hundred miles per hour during high-speed passes.

"You have to establish the ability to provide feedback to people without it being personal," he said. "So you need to be able to give feedback to somebody—constructive criticism, negative feedback, whatever you want to call it. You need to be able to do that in a setting where we all trust each other and we all know that it is for the good of the organization and that it's never personal."

While these sessions evoke extremely candid, unfiltered feedback, Armatas also underscores the importance of tact and delivery. He cites a common pitfall where some people with particularly strong personalities may say they don't care what people think and pride themselves in saying what they want to say as long as they feel it's true.

"I think that's a trap," Armatas said. "I think that you can be right, and I tell my kids this all the time. I tell them, it doesn't matter if you're right if no one's listening. I'm not saying you have to be the nicest, most likable person in the world, but if you don't do a good job of saying something the right way, then the value of the feedback is diminished by the fact no one wants to hear from you because they're upset about how it was delivered."

One way that the Blue Angels seek to ensure the most level, candid feedback during debriefs is to remove rank while doing so. When team members walk into work, yes, Commander Armatas is the boss. But when they enter the feedback room for the "after action report," everyone takes their ranks off their arms. Nobody is a general, nobody is a captain—everyone becomes equal. To Armatas and his Blue Angel predecessors, this is essential for having powerfully honest conversations where everyone can participate. It's not just the leader levying judgments; it may be the leader getting judged.

"Everything is dissected, and everybody is critiqued by everyone else," he told us. "Once you establish that trust within the organization, once we establish that none of this is personal, that we're all working together for the same common goal, then you can debrief people. You need to be a talented aviator and a capable representative of the Navy and Marine Corps. That's just to get you in the door. Your ability to have a bad day and take it in stride, as my coach used to say, that's what keeps you here. That's what allows the team to get to where it needs to get to."

W e want momentum to take us someplace. If things are working right, momentum helps lead us to success. But momentum has a shelf life. Just because there's a winning streak, it doesn't mean it'll continue at that same pace indefinitely. There are outcomes throughout a competitive experience—not just at the end of a game or the end of a quarter.

We struggled with this chapter for that reason. It would be easy to say that momentum carried a team to a spot—but the truth is that there are many spots, many games, many deals, many battles, many elections. You don't want just to live another day but to make some organization-changing transformations. We started out thinking about this chapter as relating to an "outcome," singular. But it quickly became clear that "outcome" is both too narrow and too final. We debated various other ways of imagining it—"destination" or "result," for example. But we returned to "outcomes," plural, in recognition of the countless data points, results, and inputs that individuals and teams collect along the way to a shared goal.

But at the heart of outcomes—the engine that drives what outcomes mean to a team—are the many opportunities they provide for feedback to react to. In other words, feedback is what makes outcomes meaningful in the context of momentum. This makes feedback one of the most critical components of personal and team development, serving as a guiding force for improvement, motivation, and performance evaluation. Feedback comes in various forms, each with distinct characteristics and implications for how it is received and acted upon. Understanding the diverse types and natures of feedback—including verbal, nonverbal, kinesthetic, data driven, and environmental—can significantly enhance the effectiveness of communication and performance outcomes in both individual and team contexts.

Our model of momentum depends on feedback at every level, which is why feedback—like leadership—isn't one "box" but rather a nearly all-encompassing feature, touching recruitment, spark, leadership, team climate, belief and mindset, preparation, and culture alike.

We've already looked at how important it is for teams to be receptive to clues of momentum—to be able to feel, see, and identify a spark when it's happening. Similarly, with feedback, it's critical for teams and individuals to be receptive to what constitutes feedback, which comes in many forms.

- Verbal feedback, as exemplified by the Blue Angels, is the most traditional and direct form of communication, typically involving spoken or written words that convey praise, criticism, or suggestions for improvement. This form of feedback is prevalent in educational settings, workplaces, and coaching environments. Verbal feedback can be immediate, such as in a live coaching session, or delayed, as in a written performance review. According to research, verbal feedback is most effective when it is specific, constructive, and delivered in a manner that is clear and understandable to the recipient (Hattie & Timperley, 2007). For example, a coach might say, "Your shooting form has improved, but you need to work on your foot positioning." This type of feedback provides specific information that the athlete can use to make adjustments.

- Nonverbal feedback encompasses a wide range of cues, including facial expressions, gestures, posture, and eye contact. This form of feedback often accompanies verbal communication but can also stand alone as a powerful form of expression. Nonverbal feedback is particularly significant because it can reinforce or contradict verbal messages, thereby influencing how the feedback is perceived and internalized. For instance, a team leader who nods affirmatively while a team member is speaking conveys approval and encouragement, even if they do not say anything verbally. On the other hand, crossed arms or a lack of eye contact might indicate disinterest or disagreement, even if the verbal feedback is positive. Research indicates that nonverbal communication is a critical aspect of interpersonal interactions, with some studies suggesting that it constitutes up to 93 percent of communication effectiveness in certain contexts (Mehrabian, 1971).

- Kinesthetic feedback, also known as tactile or physical feedback, involves bodily sensations and movements. This form of feedback is particularly relevant in sports, dance, and other physical activities where the body's response to movements provides immediate feedback to the performer. For example, a gymnast might feel their balance shift during a routine, prompting an immediate correction in posture. Kinesthetic feedback is often unconscious but is essential for developing motor skills and physical performance. It allows individuals to adjust their actions in real time based on the sensory information received from their bodies. Studies in motor learning suggest that kinesthetic feedback plays a crucial role in the acquisition of new skills and the refinement of existing ones (Schmidt & Lee, 2019).

- Data-driven feedback has become increasingly prominent in the digital age, utilized by businesses, political organizations, military units, and athletic teams alike. This type of feedback is derived from quantitative data, such as performance metrics, analytics, and other measurable indicators. Data-driven feedback is common in both professional and personal contexts, from business performance dashboards to fitness trackers. For teams, data-driven feedback can provide an objective basis for evaluating performance and identifying areas for improvement. For example, a sales team might receive feedback on their performance through weekly reports that show sales figures, customer satisfaction scores, and other key performance indicators. This type of feedback allows teams to make data-informed decisions and track progress over time. Data-driven feedback is valuable because it offers a level of objectivity that other forms of feedback might lack. But it is essential that the data is accurate, relevant, and presented in a way that is understandable and actionable (Pfeffer & Sutton, 2006). Additionally, combining data-driven feedback with verbal and nonverbal cues can enhance its effectiveness by providing context and meaning.

- Environmental feedback refers to the cues and information provided by one's surroundings. This type of feedback is often subtle but can significantly influence behavior and performance. For instance, the layout of a workspace, the noise level, or the availability of resources can all provide feedback about the priorities and expectations within an organization. For example, a cluttered and disorganized workspace might signal a lack of attention to detail or low organizational standards, while a well-maintained and aesthetically pleasing environment might encourage productivity and creativity. Environmental feedback can be managed strategically to create environments that support desired behaviors and outcomes (Oldham & Fried, 1987).

Successful leaders will provide opportunities for teams to collect data on performance and will train teams to identify, receive, give, and process feedback in all of its various forms. You can't lead effectively without giving and receiving feedback regularly.

Leaders rely on one key tool more than any other when driving organizational performance: influence. But influence doesn't exist in a vacuum. For leaders to know if their actions are steering the organization in the right direction, they need details. They need feedback.

The impact of feedback is hard to overstate. Gallup, the analytics powerhouse, conducted a study in 2022 that showed just how much feedback matters. Their research found that employees who received daily feedback from their managers were 3.6 times more likely to feel motivated to do exceptional work compared to those who only received feedback once a year. It's a staggering number, one that highlights how closely performance is tied to the frequency and quality of feedback.

But there's a flip side. In a 2021 Gallup poll, only 26 percent of employees strongly agreed that the feedback they received actually improved their work. This tells us something crucial: While feedback has the potential to be transformative, it's often falling short.

Why is that? A study by Megan Medvedeff, Jane B. Gregory, and Paul E. Levy offers an answer. Their research zeroed in on the kinds of feedback that really move the needle. They found that two types of feedback had the most influence on people's motivation to improve: positive outcome feedback, essentially praise for completing a task successfully, and negative process feedback, which tells someone what isn't working as they're still in the middle of a task. These two types of feedback generated the biggest boost in motivation, encouraging people to actively seek out more performance assessments.

This is where their findings really matter. Whether you're trying to build momentum or reverse a downward trend, people respond most strongly when they know they've hit the mark or when they need to course correct in the moment. It's feedback, in these forms, that can help create the spark that shifts momentum.

The takeaway here is simple: Feedback isn't just a onetime event. It's a constant, ongoing process that can propel an organization forward— or keep it from slipping backward. And without it, generating or reversing momentum becomes an impossible task. Leaders, therefore, must embrace feedback not just as a tool but as a fundamental part of organizational life.

P ost-campaign autopsy reports, also known as postmortem analyses, play a crucial role in the operations of political parties following an election. These reports serve as comprehensive evaluations of a campaign's performance, analyzing what worked, what didn't, and what could be improved in future elections. They assess the effectiveness of campaign strategies, messaging, voter outreach, and resource allocation. And a good report will also include detailed analysis of voter data, turnout patterns, and polling results to identify trends and demographic shifts that influenced the election outcome.

These reports may also provide a means of holding campaign staff, consultants, and leadership accountable for their decisions and actions during the campaign. This can lead to personnel changes or shifts in strategy. And, in some instances, particularly those that emphasize grassroots involvement, these reports may be shared with party members or the public to maintain transparency and build trust. Based on the insights gained, parties can adjust their long-term strategies, including candidate selection, policy focus, and communication methods. Insights from these reports are also used to train future candidates, campaign managers, and staff, ensuring that the party continuously evolves and improves its campaigning techniques. This type of feedback process can also serve as an important crisis management or damage control mechanism: If a campaign was particularly unsuccessful or controversial, the autopsy report can help the party manage its public image by acknowledging missteps and outlining steps for recovery.

Two contemporary, high-profile examples of campaign autopsy reports were unveiled by Republicans in 2012 following Mitt Romney's defeat to Barack Obama and by Democrats in 2016 following Hillary Clinton's loss to Donald Trump. The Republican National Committee's 2012 "Growth and Opportunity Project" was a comprehensive review to understand their loss. This report highlighted the party's need to appeal to a broader demographic, including minorities, women, and younger voters. It criticized the party's messaging and called for changes in communication strategies, particularly in engaging with Latino voters. The report also emphasized the importance of modernizing campaign infrastructure and technology.

Similarly, the Democratic National Committee's post-election analysis pointed to a range of issues, including the overreliance on data analytics over traditional campaign strategies, failure to adequately address economic anxieties in key swing states, and challenges with voter turnout. The report also critiqued the party's messaging and outreach efforts, particularly in the Midwest. The findings sparked a significant debate within the Democratic Party about its direction, messaging, and strategy, contributing to shifts in leadership and approach in the subsequent 2018 midterm elections—successfully so.

The DNC's 2016 autopsy report directly contributed to the party's investment in grassroots efforts, particularly in swing districts within states. This included expanding voter outreach, building local campaign infrastructures, and engaging more directly with communities. There was a significant push to energize and mobilize volunteers, which helped boost voter turnout and engagement in the 2018 midterms. The emphasis on grassroots organizing was a key factor in flipping many Republican-held districts.

Further, the report highlighted the need for the party to better communicate its economic message and address the concerns of working-class voters, particularly in the Midwest. For the 2018 midterms, Democrats honed their messaging around health care, the economy, and holding the Trump administration accountable, which resonated with a broader base of voters. The focus on health care, in particular, proved to be a unifying issue that helped Democrats win over voters in critical districts.

Finally, the 2016 report had pointed out deficiencies in the party's use of technology and data analytics. In response, the DNC invested in upgrading its technological infrastructure, improving voter data management, and employing more sophisticated data analytics for targeting and mobilization. This technological boost helped campaigns at all levels run more efficiently and effectively, resulting in better tools for voter engagement, including more targeted digital advertising and more efficient voter outreach efforts.

The party's investment in the postmortem—and in their willingness to receive highly critical feedback—paid off. In 2018, Democrats were able to flip forty-one House seats from Republican to Democrat, regaining control of the House of Representatives.

Douglas Stone and Sheila Heen's book, *Thanks for the Feedback*, characterized feedback as a "two-way flow that is part of every interaction." Subsequently, they identified that three primary types of feedback are involved in the flow: appreciation, coaching, and evaluation. When seeking to foster momentum, leaders will have to provide all three types of feedback and receive them as well. Most importantly, leaders are well advised to not view providing feedback as a "commonsense" practice. Learning how to properly deliver and receive feedback is an important skill set. Feedback influences the ability to foster momentum by enhancing learning or reinforcing/modifying behavior.

ACTION 1:
Provide feedback with a purpose.

It is important to "start with the end in mind." What type of feedback are you intent on providing? What are you seeking to influence?

ACTION 2:
Provide feedback with empathy and compassion.

It is possible (and important) to address challenging situations well. Remember, you manage things but lead people. Treating them with respect is fundamental. Situations where you are trying to generate positive momentum or reverse negative momentum are generally characterized by higher-than-average levels of anxiety. Effective leaders harness the components of emotional intelligence (that is, self-awareness, self-regulation, motivation, empathy, and social skill) to manage themselves and create good habits.

ACTION 3:
Understand the feedback "triggers" when you are receiving them.

Leaders absorb stress when seeking to foster momentum. Additionally, they do not always accept nonconfirmatory feedback from their teams as being valid. Stone and Heen detailed three reasons, or "triggers," that can negate our willingness to accept feedback.

Truth triggers: These are triggered by the content of the feedback itself, such as when it's untrue, unhelpful, or wrong. In response, people may feel exasperated, wronged, or indignant.

Relationship triggers: These are triggered by who gave the feedback and the relationship the recipient has with them. For example, people may react differently to feedback from people they like.

Identity triggers: These are triggered when someone feels threatened by the feedback.

There are multiple techniques leaders can leverage to overcome the triggers (for example, ask for clarification, focus on the content, manage your emotions, and look at the situation systemically).

13

When Mo Is Against You

You know those moments, though few wish to remember them. Those times when walls are closing in and everything is spiraling downward. It's the opposite sensation of the lightness, the *flow*, of momentum—but rather it's the sharp knife of when Mo is working against you or your team. During these times, the air thickens, steps feel heavier no matter how fast you try to move. The weight of failure presses from all directions, and you might question every decision you've made. The foreign yet familiar voice of failure whispers in your ear, sometimes sounding like your own voice, and doubt clouds your thoughts. The horizon gets farther and farther away.

These are the moments when a comeback might feel the hardest to contemplate. And yet—according to one person who might know more about turnaround than anyone else—these are the very moments where the path to fixing things is actually the *easiest*.

"I always like taking things on that are really, fundamentally broken," Greg Brenneman told us in a powerful interview about his experiences tackling the monster of Mo. Brenneman, a turnaround expert who has led companies like Continental Airlines and Burger King out of dire situations, knows this better than anyone. "Organizations that need a turnaround are much easier than organizations that are satisfactorily underperforming," he shared with us, and quickly, a view that had seemed paradoxical moments before now seemed clearer. "This is because, in a real crisis, everyone acknowledges the problem, and there's no resistance to change."

At Continental, where delays, lost luggage, and poor customer service were the norm, Brenneman walked into a situation where everyone knew it was bad—and that's where he thrived. "Everybody knows the way they always did it is just terrible," he reflected, which meant that the door was open to radical change.

Brenneman acknowledges that the complexity of a turnaround can be overwhelming and combats that—at least on some level—with a focused, one-page plan. For leaders walking into a struggling environment, Brenneman's first piece of advice is to create a simple, actionable plan. "You can put a one-page plan together in fourteen-point font," he advises, distilling complex strategies into focused actions. For Brenneman, this isn't about condensing a company's problems into oversimplified bullet points. It's about identifying the four or five critical areas that need attention and creating a focused, actionable road map. The genius of the one-pager is its accessibility—everyone in the organization can understand it, align with it, and act on it.

At Continental, rather than flood his team with data or elaborate strategies, the one-page plan focused attention on four key areas: market, financials, product, and people. Under each category, Brenneman outlined a few specific goals that would steer the company back on course.

The market section of the plan was dubbed "Fly to Win," a reminder to focus only on profitable routes. "Why are we flying Greensboro to Greenville eight times a day when both customers are on the first flight?" he asked. The simplicity of this approach allowed his team to quickly make critical decisions about where to focus their resources.

On the financial front, Brenneman knew Continental needed to get its house in order. "Fund the Future" became the rallying cry, a commitment to managing costs while making investments that would set the airline up for long-term success. The product section—"Make Reliability a Reality"—was Brenneman's way of telling the company to get back to basics: deliver customers to their destinations on time, with their luggage, and a good meal.

But Brenneman knew none of these changes would stick if the people weren't on board. So the final quadrant of the plan was "Work Together"—a call for unity among employees who had long been divided by distrust and internal conflict. This wasn't just about slogans—it was about tangible actions. He even introduced on-time performance bonuses to create a direct incentive for employees to care about the airline's success. Toward this goal, Brenneman emphasized to us the importance of creating small wins early. At Continental, one of his most famous initiatives was an on-time performance bonus. The company had consistently ranked last in getting flights out on time, so Brenneman offered employees a cash bonus—sixty-five dollars for ranking third and one hundred dollars for first place. The results were nearly immediate: "By month three, we were third, and by month five, we were first," Brennaman recalled to us. This not only saved the company millions in operational costs but also transformed employee morale, giving everyone tangible proof that success was possible. A simple plan had brought results almost immediately.

The beauty of Brenneman's one-pagers wasn't just their brevity—it was their clarity. Everyone, from executives to frontline employees, knew exactly what needed to be done. These plans didn't get buried in a desk drawer; they were living, breathing documents that guided decisions and inspired action. "As soon as you say something more important than what's on this page, I'm going to scratch off something on this page and put it there," Brenneman explains, underscoring his relentless focus on what truly mattered.

Another key element of reversing momentum is engaging directly with your people. Brenneman didn't just sit in the executive suite; he spent time in the trenches. "Every Friday afternoon, I'd go to the airport and spend time in the pilots' lounge, the mechanics' break room," he recounts. Building trust with employees allowed him to break down the walls between management and the workforce, fostering a culture of cooperation rather than division.

But perhaps Brenneman's most profound insight is that momentum, whether positive or negative, is powerful. He likens it to pushing a tire up a hill: "Once you got it rolling, you could just whack it every once in a while, but absolutely, one thing begets the other." Positive momentum breeds success, while negative momentum—if left unchecked—leads to further decline. "Failure can beget failure if you don't believe you can stop it," he warns. The secret lies in recognizing the small signals of change, capitalizing on early wins, and maintaining relentless focus on improvement.

For anyone facing a seemingly impossible turnaround, Brenneman offers a road map: Face the brutal facts, simplify your strategy, and involve your people in the solution. Road maps usually imply an order of things—one task after another. But when asked what leaders and teams should do first, his response doesn't offer a linear solution. At Continental, for example, Brenneman's team would ask what they should tackle first—the meals, the carpet in the terminals, baggage issues, or what.

"I would tell them, you got to do it right away and all at once, because it's all kind of cumulative.... But I always tell people, start with the five F's: faith, family, friends, fitness, finance, right?"

Momentum is never static—it's either moving with you or against you. And as Brenneman's career proves, when things are at their worst, it might be the exact right time for a leader to step in with clarity, conviction, and belief that success is within reach.

• • •

Maybe no team in the history of sports needed a reversal of momentum as desperately as the Baylor University men's basketball team. In the summer of 2003, the team made national news for all the wrong reasons. One of their players, Patrick Dennehy, went missing, and his teammate Carlos Dotson was eventually arrested and charged with Dennehy's murder. In the aftermath of that tragedy, Baylor's coach, Dave Bliss, was secretly recorded encouraging coaches to lie to investigators about the circumstances surrounding Dennehy's murder in order to cover up illegal payments Bliss was making to a number of players, among other NCAA violations. In August of that year, Bliss and the school's athletic director resigned in shame.

The team was facing severe penalties and possibly even the harshest sanction of all: the termination of the program. Historically an underperforming team, the Baylor job was now radioactive to coaches with any pedigree. But to Scott Drew, who had just completed his first season as a head coach at midmajor Valparaiso University in Indiana, it was the opportunity of a lifetime. Drew didn't just consider the job, he pursued it, sensing the chance to essentially reverse all that negativity at the largest Baptist university in the country and instill the right values from the bottom up. "Our real goal in the early years was to come from that deep place and get to a place where people would talk about Baylor without mentioning the tragedy," Drew said.

To do this, Drew and his staff did several things to eliminate the negative momentum from the previous scandal and tragedy-fueled seasons as they headed down the long road back to respectability. Respect was earned quickly, and the ultimate testament to the journey came in 2021 when the team won a national championship.

They Didn't Let Their Past
Determine Their Future

The previous coach had resigned in shame just two weeks prior and, as he took the podium to introduce himself to the college basketball world, Scott Drew had no idea how severe the penalties would be that his team would have to endure. But that didn't stop him from boldly proclaiming the reason he was there.

"At Baylor University, I did not come to go to the NCAA tournament," Drew said at his introductory press conference. "We came to win games in the NCAA tournament. We came with the chance to win a national championship at Baylor University."

There he was, a coach with just a single year of head coaching experience, none at the major college level, taking the reins of the least desirable job in America and declaring the ultimate vision. Scott Drew and Baylor might not have made it to the ultimate mountaintop until a number of years later, but the first step on that championship journey began with the words he spoke, and the vision he cast.

They Preached Their Values
from Day One

When he took over a team in complete disrepair, one of the first things Drew did at Baylor was to implement team chapel services before every home game. The team chaplain had never been asked to do anything like that before, but Drew was adamant that the team not only needed regular instruction on how to perform and improve on the court, but they needed guidance and inspiration off it as well.

One of the issues the Baylor team dealt with was substance abuse, brought on in part by Baylor's historic willingness to use fake drug test results to keep players eligible. Drew and his staff told players there

252

would be no tolerance for illegal drugs. But they also said there would be no profanity used either, and any violations of that rule would be punished with push-ups. They also said that, as a staff, they would hold themselves to the same standard.

In their last game of the season against Oklahoma, Scott Drew was trying to fire up his team to match their opponent's physicality. "We need to keep their asses off the boards," the notoriously choirboy clean Drew screamed. "And I will do push-ups for that!" His team went wild.

They finished their season in a close loss that night, but the message was sent, and the culture was turning.

They Celebrated Wins, No Matter How Small

Baylor lost that first season—and lost big. But Scott Drew and his staff were still able to create moments, and celebrate them, when the tide started to turn. Down by 40 to powerhouse Kansas late in the game, Scott Drew challenged his players to win the last four minutes. When Baylor made a hustle basket in the last few seconds to accomplish the goal, "we celebrated on the bench like we just won the national title," Drew told us. "The crowd thought we were nuts. But we were building something."

The team would only win three conference games all season, but the coaches championed each one. They had a big whiteboard in their locker room, and when they won their first Big 12 game, they drew a huge "1" on it. When they beat Texas A&M for just their second win, the coaches made a big deal about erasing it, and putting a "2" on it. By the time they won their third, and final, conference game of the season, the players had taken over marker duties. The players were not just celebrating the wins but engaging in the cultural practices the coaches had created.

The NCAA extended Baylor's postseason sanctions for Drew's first years in Waco. But through persistent optimism, consistent effort, and a disciplined adherence to the values and vision they set down on day one, the prophecy Drew preached at his initial press conference eventually came true.

Winston Churchill is claimed to have said, "Success is not final, failure is not fatal: it's the courage to continue that counts." So it is true with momentum. By its very definition, momentum is impermanent—and measured really only against the context of periods of stasis, stability, or, in some cases, decline.

Ups, in other words, are measured against flat roads or slumps, pains against some individual baseline of comfort. And to companies in the midst of an industry-wide crisis, success may also be a relative term. Certainly, to Lumen CEO Kate Johnson—who was brought in to transform the company during a period in which all tech companies were facing common threats—her starting goal was to change the goal itself.

In the fast-paced, unforgiving world of technology and telecommunications, Lumen Technologies found itself at a critical juncture. Once a titan in the industry, known for its extensive network infrastructure and innovative solutions, Lumen faced a daunting reality: The company was losing its competitive edge. Market share was slipping, customer satisfaction was dwindling, and the once-unstoppable momentum had come to a grinding halt. Lumen's struggles were not sudden but rather a slow, painful descent. The company, formerly known as CenturyLink, had expanded rapidly through acquisitions, including the high-profile purchases of Level 3 Communications in 2017 and Qwest Communications in 2011. While these moves initially bolstered Lumen's network capabilities and market presence, they also brought about significant integration challenges. The sheer scale of merging disparate systems and cultures proved overwhelming.

Internally, morale was low. Employees were disillusioned by constant restructuring, and the lack of a cohesive vision led to inefficiencies. Externally, customers were frustrated. Service disruptions became commonplace, and the once-stellar reputation for reliability and innovation was tarnished. Competitors such as AT&T and Verizon seized the opportunity, leveraging their agility to outmaneuver Lumen in critical markets. It seemed as though the company's best days were behind it.

When Johnson was hired, Lumen had been operating on the principle of "you want to lose last," she told us. "In a declining market, you've got secular headwinds, and everybody's revenue is declining on that old copper [wire] base, and you want to keep paying a dividend. You want to lose last. You want to be the last company standing." But that wasn't what Johnson had in mind.

"That was not my assignment," Johnson was clear. "In November of 2022 the board of Lumen hired me to transform the company. We agreed. The only way to do that was to pivot to growth. We had to cut the dividend, and we had to set up a new mission and a new strategy, a new operating plan, and a completely new leadership team in order to get value from the fiber network that we knew was coming. We saw some tailwinds that would be very accretive to the story, but you know, when you think about how I'm leading the company versus prior administrations, it's really an apple and an orange."

Johnson's appointment marked a pivotal moment. Johnson, who had left her position as president of Microsoft US in 2021, brought a fresh perspective and an unwavering resolve to steer Lumen out of its quagmire. She had taken a sabbatical between jobs—focusing her attention on leadership and mindfulness courses, tapping more deeply into the spiritual basis for what her purpose was, and how she could best serve. Consistent with this type of discipline and intention, Johnson's initial days were spent listening. She conducted a thorough assessment of the company's strengths and weaknesses, engaging with employees at all levels. Her approach was holistic, recognizing that the key to reversing Lumen's fortunes lay not just in technological advancements but in reigniting the human spirit within the organization. "Well, it starts with them, right?" Johnson reflected to us. "Because, you know, they're the ones that wake up every day and make a decision. Am I gonna do it the old way, or am I gonna lean into the new way? The new way is scary. I might make a mistake. I might feel awkward. I might be embarrassed. But, you know, I gotta dive into it. I've gotta use this sort of systemic resilience we're trying to build."

Johnson's approach included "city swings," where she would travel to different Lumen locations, immersing herself in local operations and meeting with employees, customers, analysts, and partners to understand their challenges and perspectives. "It's very formulaic," Johnson explained. "It's a couple of days. And it's these immersions."

She'd also spend time at home base conducting employee forums, where she'd go layer by layer spending time with leadership. "Tell me everything," she would say. "How are you thinking about my joining? How are you thinking about our new mission? How are you thinking about where we are?" And the teams would let Johnson see through their respective lenses. "You have to go all the way through the director community, the manager community, and the individual contributor community to get the full story. And I started with really small groups, six to ten people," she told us, eventually building up to forums that would include thirty to fifty employees at a time.

Johnson would speak at these, too, in part to demonstrate vulnerability in order to build comfort and trust. "At first, when you're a new CEO and you come in and you have, you know, six to ten directors, they're like, I'm not gonna tell you what I'm actually thinking, like this is terrifying," she said. "But you demonstrate. You know, you get in the right mindset; you get curious. You share mistakes you've made, you own up to it, and you try and create a space that encourages bravery, the courage to tell you the truth, to speak truth to power." It isn't always easy, and Johnson knows that going in—not easy on the employees, and not always easy on her.

"They're very courageous, and I always have to sort of like drink a tall glass of optimism before I go in, because I'm gonna get the truth. And the truth is hard. You know, our systems aren't there yet. Our processes aren't there yet. We're in the middle of one of the more complicated corporate turnarounds in history. I believe deeply in my heart we're gonna win, but it's hard. And you have to be willing to hear the hard truths. Though you know X, Y, and Z are working well, P, D, and Q are still not. And you have to take your breath and say one thing at a time. Stay with me, guys, you know we're gonna knock these things out. And they see the progress on one side, and then they get the courage to bring the next thing to you. But you know it can be, it could be, a little tiring and could be a little exhausting, right? But that's how I do it. I have these forums where I do my deep dives."

After her initial and ongoing deep dives to continually understand, map, and interpret challenges, Johnson shared with us the ensuing elements of her turnaround strategy.

1. *Give concise feedback:* Johnson's personal life—her marriage and her athletics—have guided her approach to management. She never offers more than three things for someone to work on at any one time. "I don't think you can work on more than three," she shared with us. "Now, that said, if my senior leadership team were here, they'd be like, well, then, why are we working on five priorities. And it's a good

question. It's fair. But we need to do those five things. So, yeah, I think three is the magic number for changing your own game. If you take five or seven priorities, whatever the number is, and you sprinkle them around the company, I hope that nobody's working on more than three of those individually."

2.   *Be in the point, not in the match:* Johnson thinks back on a high-stakes doubles match where she became emotionally vulnerable to negative momentum. "I kind of lost sight of momentum as soon as we lost a couple of points," she said. "I forgot about our winning momentum and went right into this losing momentum story in my head, and I kept thinking about winning the match and my partner. You know, we were sort of at the high level, thinking about the win versus the loss instead of 'I gotta win this point right now.' And this is the best way to go about that—that anchoring in winning one point at a time is deeply relevant to business, as is this notion of momentum and inertia." In business, it isn't as easy as it sounds to stay grounded in the point rather than the match. "It really isn't easy. And, you know, I mean, the emotional dynamics especially. Look, we're transforming a company, and we're disrupting an industry. It's a battleground. We're competing with some of the biggest and best companies in the world to try and take share and change outcomes for customers. And it's not just the strategy. It's not just the operating plan and the execution. It's not just the talent or the skills or the systems of the process. It's managing the emotional dynamics of a battleground and staying focused

on what's going to make the biggest impact. That's the job. And it's really hard."

3. *Get close and tell a story:* Johnson believes it's impossible to "really empathize with a human or an issue or a problem unless you get really close to it" and that it's "important for leadership to be okay with diving all the way down into it, so you can deeply understand it. And that's not something that a lot of leaders do." Johnson thinks that when most leaders "escape the ranks of level 1, 2, 3, 4, and they're up in the 7 to 8 atmosphere, they forget to go back." Johnson recommends that leaders get close to these problems, get close to your people, and once there focus on the power of storytelling: "If you wanna be a great commercial force in any industry, the art of storytelling is critical. There's gotta be a problem. There's gotta be a climax, and there's gotta be an outcome and resolution. And if you can, embed that in how customers use and gain value from your products and services."

4. *Be silly, and optimistic:* "I'm telling them something that I see that their management chain hasn't told them yet. Something positive. It's also delivering the excitement and the energy and the hope and the optimism back to them." Johnson shared with us one particularly memorable story: "I love scooters, right? And I had several of them in my office, and I use them to disarm people. I say, 'Hey. You wanna go for a scooter ride around the office?' and people are like, 'Is she crazy?' No. Actually, I am a little bit crazy, but if you're riding around on a scooter, it is almost

impossible to take yourself too seriously. And that's the trick, right?" Johnson didn't reserve this tactic for staff only but for others who came into her orbit—including longtime Seattle Seahawks coach Pete Carroll, during their first encounter at Microsoft. Before even a handshake, Johnson invited Carroll to a scooter race, and he was all in. Johnson, in heels, may have seemed like an easy win for Carroll, who warned her in advance, "No whining!" But Johnson had no intention of being in such a position. "I started zooming down the hallway, and I figured, he's a football coach so full contact isn't a problem, right? So I used every imaginable technique to win that race. And I'm not going to tell you who won or lost. I will tell you that there were several wipeouts and a lot of laughing along the way." Employees from their respective cubicles and offices looked on. About a hundred were in the office at the time. And there's Pete Carroll zooming through the halls of Microsoft, on a scooter. "OSHA was not thrilled," Johnson said, laughing.

5. *Cross-pollinate:* Johnson put people in cross-functional groups and insisted upon setting aside time for team members to get to know one another. "My leadership team was brand new, which was kind of a big deal. In order to accelerate relationships, which take time to develop, we allocate time to be in person every month and, within these meetings, dedicate time toward relationship development." Johnson initiated personality tests where team members shared results, talking about family, and preferences, and life. "Everybody's got these crazy things going on in their lives. We make space to bring them in, in whatever way

they're comfortable. We don't mandate that you have to tell some sort of secret. You set up your own boundaries, but give us a look at where you are in life and journey." Johnson shares how she would talk to team members. "Why'd you come to Lumen? How does it fit into your life story? Tell us one thing that's super interesting."

Though the word had been said a number of times, and the theme was felt throughout, it wasn't until late in our conversation that we asked Kate about momentum.

"Is it real?" we asked.

"That's a hard yes," Johnson replied, without hesitation. "First of all, I have an electrical engineering degree. I've taken many physics classes. I love physics. That explains how the universe works. In a transformation, inertia and momentum are incredibly important. You know, the sort of the Newtonian laws of motion: Objects in motion stay in motion; objects at rest stay at rest unless there's an external force. My belief is that the translation of those sets of laws to corporate America is that companies that are winning stay winning, and companies that are losing stay losing unless there's some external force, and the external force at Lumen in our industry is our transformation. We're getting the people and the talent; we're getting a system refresh. We're redesigning our processes. We're redesigning the value that we bring to customers. So that's external force number one. External force number two is this unprecedented spike in demand for terrestrial internet. Right now we're prepared to capture that opportunity. Momentum is mass times velocity. I need more velocity, and we're a twenty-five-thousand-person mass company.

They gotta lean in with me so that we can increase that number and go faster."

Few things captivate sports fans more than the thrill of an underdog story or an unlikely comeback. The energy in the arena becomes palpable, the crowd's belief in an impending victory surges, and the narrative of momentum takes center stage. This phenomenon isn't confined to sports alone; it echoes in politics, military history, and the business world, where a sudden reversal of fortunes is often seen as the result of an unstoppable momentum.

How does a team, on the precipice of defeat, become the team that stuns observers and full throttles into victory? We concede that in the thousands of journal articles we've read on this topic, science has struggled to identify the variables that make momentum more or less likely. One 2019 study by Israeli researchers in the *Journal of Economic Psychology* stands out as particularly interesting. They wanted to know whether NBA teams that clawed their way back to a tie in regulation time had a higher chance of winning in overtime. In other words, did the last-minute tie that led to extra minutes result in psychological momentum that drove the come-from-behind team to a win? Their statistical models didn't find that to be the case. But what their results did uncover is a variety of variables that did drive success: home court advantage, for example, where the energy of crowds contributes to a team's drive, and the team's season record, where sustained levels of high performance built upon itself. Their study also stands out as one that deserves a follow-up study—one that doesn't use a final score win as the dependent variable of interest but, rather, looks at the factors that led the losing team to achieve a comeback great enough to lead to overtime to begin with.

In this book, we recognize that the final score matters, but equally so, we are interested in understanding how a team that's struggling finds itself able to rally, improve, and seize a moment. The "final" outcome may leave them a point or two short of a *W* in a particular battle, but it is the bigger picture that matters just as much. Of course, final *W*'s matter too. Consider the 2004 American League Championship Series where the Boston Red Sox, down 3–0 to the New York Yankees, staged one of the most remarkable comebacks in sports history. The team's dynamics, strategic decisions, and adjustments made during the series primed them for this surge. The psychological boost from each win reinforced their belief, creating a self-fulfilling cycle where momentum became more than just a feeling—it became a force that was tactically leveraged.

This concept extends beyond sports. In the 1948 US presidential election, Harry Truman's unexpected victory over Thomas Dewey is also attributed to his relentless campaign momentum. And this momentum wasn't merely an accident. Truman's team tapped into emerging voter sentiments, adjusted their strategies to capitalize on Dewey's complacency, and effectively communicated a message that resonated with a fragmented electorate. What looked to the world like a natural wave of support was rooted not in chance but in the deliberate, strategic choices Truman and his team made.

In military history, the Battle of Midway is often cited as a pivotal moment in World War II, where momentum shifted decisively in favor of the Allied forces. Once again, this turnaround was the result of deliberate intelligence operations, strategic decisions, and tactical executions that set the stage for this shift. The momentum that followed was not just a consequence of these actions but was, in part, created by them.

Similarly, in the business world, Apple's resurgence under Steve Jobs is frequently described as a momentum-driven comeback. And once again, the momentum witnessed by observers was not simply by chance. Apple's resurgence was carefully cultivated through innovation, strategic leadership, and the ability to capture the zeitgeist of the early twenty-first century. The introduction of the iPod, and later the iPhone, didn't just ride a wave of consumer interest—they created it, fueling a momentum that propelled Apple to unprecedented heights.

In other words, teams, leaders, and organizations that successfully harness momentum do so by understanding and manipulating the conditions that allow it to flourish. The result may look effortless to observers—and, in the moment of a surge, may in fact feel effortless to the "players" too—but make no mistake, the often-hidden factors behind a reversal in momentum are born out of preparation, mindset, team climate, and leadership that together recognize and act upon a spark.

About the Authors

DON YAEGER is a twelve-time *New York Times* bestselling author, longtime associate editor at *Sports Illustrated*, and today one of the most in-demand public speakers on the corporate circuit. He delivers seventy speeches a year to an average annual audience of one hundred thousand people. He lives in Tallahassee, Florida, with his wife and two children. He is the host of the highly rated *Corporate Competitor Podcast* and offers training courses developed from his years of research into high-performance habits. Learn more at www.donyaeger.com.

BERNIE BANKS is the director of Rice University's Doerr Institute for New Leaders and a professor in the practice of leadership within the university's Jesse H. Jones Graduate School of Business. Bernie retired from the US Army in 2016 as a brigadier general after having successfully led West Point's Department of Behavioral Sciences & Leadership in his final assignment. He has led multiple military units ranging in size from ten to more than three thousand people. Additionally, Bernie has engaged with organizations around the globe regarding their leader development efforts.